EATING AND DRINKING IN

Italy

Andy Herbach

OPEN ROAD PUBLISHING

OPEN ROAD PUBLISHING

www.openroadguides.com

Eighth Edition

Copyright © 2017 by Andy Herbach and Michael Dillon
- All Rights Reserved -

Illustrations: Michael Dillon
Updated by Andy Herbach

Library of Congress Control No. 2016962750
ISBN: 9781593602260

The authors have made every effort to be as accurate as possible, but neither they nor the publisher assume responsibility for the services provided by any business listed in this guide; for any errors or omissions; or any loss, damage or disruptions in your travels for any reason.

Table of Contents

Introduction

Can you imagine a foreign traveler who speaks basic English understanding what prime rib is? Or a porterhouse? Veggie platter, anyone? Buffalo wings? Sloppy joes?

Even people who speak passable Italian can have trouble reading a menu. You may know *ricotta* cheese, but not *malfatti di ricotta* which means "badly made," a reference to the handmade dumpling with *ricotta* cheese filling. You may be surprised to find *puttanesca* (which means *in the style of a prostitute*) on the menu. It's a sauce of tomatoes, capers, anchovies, black olives and garlic.

Understanding the customs and food of a country helps travelers understand the people who live in the country.

If you love to travel as we do, you know the importance of a good guide. The same is true of dining. A good guide can make all the difference between a memorable evening and a dizzyingly bad one. This guide will help you find your way around a menu written in Italian. It gives you the freedom to enter places you might never have before and order a dinner without shouting, pointing and hand waving. Instead of fumbling with a bulky, conspicuous tourist guide (most of which usually include a very incomplete listing of foods) in a restaurant, this book is a pocket-sized alphabetical listing of food and drink commonly found on menus in Italy.

Although, now that we think about it, a dinner without shouting and hand waving is not truly Italian.

6

Of course, traveling to a foreign country means something different to everyone. For every vacation there are different expectations, different needs, and every traveler has his or her own idea of what will make that vacation memorable. For us, the making of a memorable vacation begins and ends with food.

We spent the morning staring at the Sistine Chapel and the Vatican Museum, but what stands out in our minds is the wonderful lunch in the *trattoria* afterward. The creamy shrimp pasta dish was as heavenly as Michelangelo's masterpiece. We spent a morning driving to see the Leaning Tower of Pisa, but the grilled lamb in Lerici made the day.

We know the panic of opening a menu without recognizing one word on it and the disappointment of being served something other than what you thought you'd ordered. On our first trip to Europe, we were served a plate of cold brains; we thought we had ordered chicken. This guide was created for the traveler who wants to enjoy, appreciate and experience authentic cuisine *and* know what he or she is eating.

The next time you find yourself seated in a red-tiled courtyard with the scent of simmering garlic in the night air and an incomprehensible menu in your hands, simply pull this guide from your pocket and get ready to enjoy the delicious cuisine of Italy.

In Italy and Ticino (the Italian-speaking region of Switzerland), the menu is almost always posted outside of the restaurant or in a window. This makes choosing a restaurant easy and fun as you "window shop" for your next meal.

Remember that the dish that you ordered may not be exactly as described in this guide. Every chef is (and should be) innovative. What we have listed for you in this guide is the most common version of a dish.

If a menu has an English translation it does not mean that the translation is correct.

In Italy, it's customary to order a first course (pasta, rice or soup), a second course (meat, poultry or fish) and a side dish (salad, potato or vegetable). Rarely does an Italian order only a first course (such as ordering only pasta), but that doesn't mean you can't.

Tipping

A service charge is almost always added to your bill (*il conto*) in Italy. Depending on the service, it's sometimes appropriate to leave up to 5%. Most locals round up to the next euro and it's okay if that is what you do, too. Travelers from the U.S. sometimes have trouble *not* tipping. Remember, you do *not* have to tip. The menu will usually note that service is included (*servizio incluso* or *servizio compreso*).

You will often find *coperto* or cover charge on your menu (a charge just for placing your butt at the table). This flat fee is usually between one euro to three euros per person.

Mealtimes

In northern Italy, lunch is served from noon to around 2 p.m., and dinner from 7 p.m. to 10 p.m. In the south, lunch is served from 1 p.m. and dinner from 8 p.m. No "early bird special" in Italy. Ticino's hours are the same as in northern Italy.

Europeans joke that you can tell a U.S. tourist from his fanny pack, clothes and ubiquitous bottle of mineral water. Tap water is safe in Italy and Switzerland. Occasionally, you will find *non potabile* signs in rest rooms (especially in the rest stops of highways). This means that the water is not safe for drinking.

Waiters and waitresses will often bring *acqua minerale* (mineral water) to your table. You will be charged for it, so if you do not want mineral water ask for *acqua semplice* or *acqua di rubinetto* (tap water).

Restaurants in This Guide

Each of our recommended restaurants offers something different. Some have great food and little ambiance. Others have great ambiance and adequate food. Still others have both. Our goal is to find restaurants that are moderately priced and enjoyable. All restaurants have been tried and tested. Not enough can be said for a friendly welcome and great service. No matter how fabulous the meal, the experience will always be better when the staff treats you as if they actually want you there rather than simply tolerating your presence.

Times can change and restaurants can close, so do a walk-by earlier in the day or the day before, if possible. Our full list of restaurants starting on page 99 includes many of the eating establishments listed below.

Types of Eating Establishments

Bacaro: Venetian wine bar serving snacks like Spanish *tapas*.
Bar: Bars serve espresso, cappuccino, rolls, small sandwiches, alcoholic beverages and soft drinks.
Bottiglieria: Simple drinking establishments with limited menus but plenty of bottles of wine. Originally, these "bottle shops" served only liquor. Also called *fiaschetteria*, *cantina* or *trani*.
Enoteca: Wine bar.
Gelateria: Shop serving *gelato* (ice cream).
Grotta: Ticino has many *grotte*. These are village restaurants that take their name from caves used to store food and wine. Originally, a *grotta* was a simple eating establishment, but today many are quite expensive with extensive menus.
Locanda: Found in the country, serves regional meats and seafood.

Osteria: A tavern or wine shop. This name has also come to refer to a restaurant. These can also be called *cucina* or *hostaria*.

Paninoteca: Usually serves only sandwiches.

Pasticceria: Pastry shop.

Pizza Rustica: Common in central Italy; serves large rectangular pizzas with thicker crusts and more toppings than usually found in a *pizzeria*. You can order as much as you want, and pay by weight.

Pizzeria: We think you can figure this one out.

Ristorante: A restaurant.

Rosticceria: A deli, sometimes with a few tables, where you can order grilled meats (especially chicken).

Tavola Calda: Small restaurant with take-out or fast foods and usually with a few tables.

Trattoria: Less expensive family-run restaurant, usually not too fancy.

Tips for Budget Dining in Italy

There is no need to spend a lot of money in Italy to eat good food. There are all kinds of fabulous foods to be had inexpensively all over Italy.

Eat at a neighborhood restaurant or *trattoria*. You'll always know the price of a meal before entering, as almost all restaurants in Italy post the menu and prices in the window. Never order anything whose price is not known in advance. For instance, if you see *etto* on a menu in Venice this means that you're paying by weight (an *etto* is 100 grams), which can be extremely expensive.

Delis and food stores can provide cheap and wonderful meals. Buy cheese, bread, wine and other snacks and have a picnic. Remember to pack a corkscrew and eating utensils when you leave home.

Lunch, even at the most expensive restaurants listed in this guide, always has a lower price. So, have lunch as your main meal.

Restaurants that have menus written in English (especially those near tourist attractions) are almost always more expensive than neighborhood restaurants.

Street vendors generally sell inexpensive and good food. For the cost of a cup of coffee or a drink, you can linger at a café and watch the world pass you by for as long as you want. It's one of Italy's greatest bargains.

And don't eat at McDonald's, for God's sake.

Speaking Italian - Pronunciation Guide

If you're looking for a comprehensive guide to speaking Italian, this is not the the place. These are simply a few tips for speaking Italian followed by a very brief pronunciation guide. It's always good to learn a few polite terms so that you can excuse yourself when you've stepped on the foot of an elderly lady or spilled your drink down the back of the gentleman in front of you. It's also just common courtesy to greet the people you meet in your hotel, and in shops and restaurants, in their own language.

In Italian, you pronounce every letter. E and i are soft vowels when used with consonants. The final e is always pronounced.

The second to the last syllable is stressed. If there is an accent in the word, stress the accented syllable.

a like in father.
au like ow in cow.
b the same as in English.
c **ca, co** and **cu** like k in keep.
– **ce** and **ci**, like ch in cheap.
ch like k in kite.
d the same as in English.
e like in day.
ei like ay in lay.
f the same as in English.
g **ga, go** and **gu** like g in gate.
– **ge** and **gi** like j in jar.
gh like g in goat.
gl like gl in glow except before i, then like lli in million.
gn like ni in onion.
h silent. H after a consonant gives it a hard sound.
i like ee in jeep.
ie, io, iu, **i** is pronounced as y (ie. *pensione* ~ pen syo neh).
k/l/m/n the same as in English.
o usually like o in boat.
p/q the same as in English.

ue, ui, uo, the u is pronounced like a w (ie. *buono* ~ bwo no).
r with a slight trill.
s like s in sit except between two vowels, then like s in hose.
sc **sca, sco** or **scu** as sk in skirt.
– **sce** or **sci** as sh in sharp.
t the same as English.
u like oo in foot.
v the same as in English.
z the same as ds in fads.

Pronunciation
_____

CA – KA
CE – CHAY
CI – CHEE
CHI – KEY
CHE – KAY

Confused?

11

~& ITALY &~

ABRUZZO & MOLISE
(Off-the-Beaten-Track Italy)

Along the Adriatic coast are
the mountainous regions
of Abruzzo and Molise. The
quiet hill towns are in great
contrast to the Adriatic resorts.
The most notable tourist venue is
the Abruzzo National Park, a place
for hikers and nature lovers. Outside this
nature reserve is Scanno, a popular summer resort town. L`Aquila (which means
"the eagle") is the capital of Abruzzo
and is a business center. Few tourists
from the United States and Canada
visit this part of Italy. If you're looking
for off-the-beaten-track destinations
and mountain scenery, Molise and
Abruzzo will certainly please.

Inland, you will find menus dominated by *capretto* (baby
goat), *agnello arrosto* (roast lamb), and *porchetta* (roast pig). On
the coast (in restaurants not serving tourist fare) try *brodetto*
(fish soup). *Centerbe* (a green herb liquor) accompanies
many meals. For dessert, try *confetti* (flower-shaped
candy made from sugar-coated almonds).

APULIA (The "Heel" of Italy)

Apulia (Puglia) is the "heel" of Italy. Oppressively hot in July
and August, a rainy day is rare. Apulia is a large wine-producing
region. The area is not frequented by many North American tourists. The baroque town of Martina Franca and the whitewashed
town of Locorotondo are in the wine region and worth a visit. Part
of the coast is heavily industrialized with immense steelworks.
12

Bari is a modern port and a common departure point for travelers to Greece. *Trulli*, dome-shaped whitewashed stone buildings, are indigenous to the area. The largest collection of *trulli* can be found near Alberobello. The Adriatic fishing ports have architecture similar to the old Venetian ports. Taranto is a modern town, as is the important port of Brindisi, another frequent departure point for visits to Greece. Not to be missed is the lovely Baroque town of Lecce.

Focaccia barese (stuffed pizza), often with *burrata* (very buttery cheese), *triglia* (red mullet), *spigola* (sea bass), *orecchiette con le cime di rapa* (ear-shaped pasta with turnips) and *tiella di riso e cozze* (a mussels, rice and potato dish) can all be found on Apulia's menus. Some avoid the *polpi arricciati* ("curled octopus") when they see that the octopus is beaten and twirled in a basket in order to get the desired "curled" shape. *Bianco di Martina* is a common fortified wine found in Apulia.

BASILICATA
(Undiscovered Italy)

This area was once known as Lucania. One of Italy's smallest regions, Basilicata is also its poorest. Mountainous and barren, Basilicata is not visited by many tourists. The capital city of Potenza was badly damaged in a 1980's earthquake. The hill town of Maratea is dramatically situated on the coast. Here, in small villages such as Metaponto and Matera, you experience the simple Italy.

Spicy *sugna piccante* (pork sauce) flavors many dishes. *Maiale* (pork) is found on most menus, and cured meats like the sausage *luganega*, *luganica* or *lucanica* (there are even

13

Friuli-Venezia Giulia

Veneto

San Marino

Le Marche

Abruzzo

Molise

Apulia

Campania

Basilicata

Calabria

Sicily

more spellings than this!) are common. *Peperoncini* (small hot green peppers preserved in oil) are added to many dishes. Try *scamorza* cheese (the local version of aged *mozzarella*).

CALABRIA (The "Toe" of Italy)

Sun, white-sand beaches, rugged mountains, olive groves and the huge rock of Scilla are all found on the "toe" of Italy. The area was once known as Magna Graecia, and there are villages where a Greek dialect is still spoken. The mountain towns such as Serra San Bruno remain as they were several hundred years ago. Rossano is a beautiful medieval town overlooking a great ravine. Consenza is a town built on a steep hillside with an interesting (almost dilapidated) look to it. Many tourists find themselves in modern Reggio on their way to Sicily. The small towns of Pizzo and Tropea are worth a visit to experience the true Calabria. We would be remiss if we did not mention that some areas of Calabria are strongholds of the local mafia and not recommended for travel.

Costolette d'agnello (lamb chops) and *pesce spada* (swordfish) are found on most menus. *Novellame* is a spread of salted anchovies and *peperoncino* sauce. Pasta is often served with chickpeas (*ceci*). *Stracotto* is a beef stew which in Calabria includes carrots, mushrooms, onions, nutmeg and cloves. *Caviale del sud* or "caviar of the south" is a dish of fried fish preserved in oil and powdered with *peperoncino*. *Fichi* (figs) are featured in many desserts.

CAMPANIA (Naples, Capri & the Amalfi Coast)

Naples, in the shadow of Vesuvius, is congested, noisy, has a reputation as dangerous, and is not an easy city for the tourist. After a quick view of Naples' old town along the harbor, most head for the nearby ruins of Herculaneum and Pompeii. It's an eerie experience walking through nearly perfectly preserved ancient communities buried by the volcanic eruption of Vesuvius. The volcanic island of Ischia and nearby Capri are

often overrun by day trippers in high season. Although it can be expensive, Capri (with its breathtaking vistas) remains the favorite of many returning visitors. The gateway to the Amalfi coast is Sorrento, perched over the sea. The Amalfi coast is the most spectacular coastal drive in Italy (if you have the nerve to drive it in high season). Positano has a great beach with a view of the town perched on the bluff. Amalfi and Ravello, further down the Amalfi coast, have spectacular views. The Amalfi coast reigns as one of the most scenic and photographed coasts in the world.

Seafood is prevalent along the coast, especially *polpi affogati* (octopus in a spicy tomato sauce). Pizza, said to have originated in Naples, is found in many varieties. *Pizza alla Napoletana* is pizza with tomato sauce and anchovies. You will eat tomatoes here like you have never had before. Many pasta dishes are served *al pomodoro* (with a tomato sauce). Meat is often cooked *alla pizzaiola* (in a tomato sauce with garlic). *Partenopea* on a menu simply means served Naples style. For dessert try *sfogliatella* (flaky pastry filled with sweet *ricotta* cheese).

EMILIA-ROMAGNA (From the Adriatic Sea to Central Italy)

The Romans built a grand road from Rimini on the Adriatic Sea to Piacenza in central Italy. The towns that now make up this region developed along this road, the Via Emilia. Piacenza is a major industrial city with a lovely downtown. Parma (which lends its name to the famous Parma ham or *prosciutto*), Modena (home to the Ferrari and Maserati automobiles), Bologna (a learning center, important city for commerce, and *the* food town in Italy), and Ferrara (less spoiled by modern times than the others) are all towns with important historic centers. Imposing Ravenna is in contrast to the most popular Adriatic resort of Rimini. Be careful, as Rimini can be quite dull, even completely closed, off season and extremely overcrowded in season.

The coast features *brodetto* (fish soup). *Prosciutto di Parma* (Parma ham) is common as is *risotto* (the famous Italian rice dish). Suckling pig is called *lattonzolo* here. For dessert, try *castagnole* (chestnut fritters). True Italian food is rare in Rimini, which has revised its menus to cater to the European package tourist.

FRIULI-VENEZIA GIULIA (Trieste & the Austrian Border)

This region borders on Austria and Slovenia. Udine is the capital but Trieste draws the most attention. Trieste, which remained under United Nations control until 1954, is an interesting mix of Austrian and Italian with a Slavic influence from the former Yugoslav republics. The architecture along the port demonstrates the mix of rulers in Trieste. Our several trips to Trieste have made us realize that this area is often, unfortunately, overlooked by tourists. White wine is produced in the hills of Friuli-Venezia Giulia. Visit the towns of Colli Orientali and Collio. The small mountain towns along the Austrian border allow the visitor to experience a mixture of Italy and Austria.

Jota is a minestrone found here and usually contains sauerkraut. *Polenta* (cornmeal mush) is found everywhere. *Brodetto* (fish soup) is common in the coastal area of this region. *Cialzons* is a sweet-and-sour pasta dish found here. The town of San Daniele is the home of *prosciutto di San Daniele* (a cured ham). The Slavic influence is found in the Trieste dessert of *gubana* (sweet bread roll) and the Austrian influence is found in the many coffeehouses of Trieste.

LAZIO (Rome & its Environs)

Lazio (also called Latium) is the region around Rome. To try to list Rome's main attractions would require another guide. Rome can be a frustrating city (it can be hard to carry on a conversation while walking down the street due to the constant traffic noise).

But, difficulties aside, few places in the world have so many important sites in such a small area, including the Vatican with its Sistine Chapel, Circus Maximus, the Spanish Steps, the Trevi Fountain, the catacombs...

Sperlonga, San Felice Circeo, Santa Severa and Santa Marinella are all coastal towns worth a visit. Ostia is a large coastal city near Rome and was the main Roman port. Its impressive ruins are an easy day trip from Rome. In inland Lazio, you may visit Tivoli (with Hadrian's Villa), Palestrina, the mountain town of Subiaco and the walled town of Viterbo.

Rome is said to have 5,000 restaurants where you can eat just about anything. After a grueling day of sightseeing, stop in a small restaurant (*trattoria*), drink some wine and eat a hearty dish of pasta such as one served *all' arrabbiata* (in a spicy tomato and herb sauce) or *alla carbonara* (with bacon, cheese, olive oil and eggs). Meals often start with *bruschetta* (garlic toast) and end with *grappa* (of which we drank a little too much on our first night here). When in Rome...

LE MARCHE (The Apennines Mountain Region)

The Apennines Mountains separate Le Marche from the rest of Central Italy. Ancona, on the Adriatic coast (a common departure point for Venice) is a modern port town. Pilgrims visit the house of the Virgin Mary in Loreto (brought here, according to legend, by angels). Urbino, one of the lesser-known great Renaissance cities, looks much as it did in the fifteenth century. In the Tronto River Valley, scenic Ascoli Piceno is another Le Marche town worth visiting. Most travelers head for the crowded (package tour-filled) coastal towns. These crowded resorts are in great contrast to the sedate hill towns.

Truffles (*tartufi*) are a specialty here, and summer peaches (*pesche*) and plums (*susine*) are some of the best fruits you will ever taste. *Vincigrassi* (baked lasagna dish), *olive all'ascolana* (large stuffed olives), *porchetta* (roast suckling pig) and rabbit (*coniglio)* are popular. *Brodetto di pesce* (fish soup) is found along the coast. In Ancona, *brodetto* contains thirteen varieties of fish.

LIGURIA (The Italian Riviera)

Wedged between mountains and the sea, the coastal region of Liguria stretches from the French border to Tuscany and is a popular tourist destination. Genoa, a large industrial city, is also Italy's biggest port. Tourists usually visit only the old, central part of the city. West of Genoa toward the French border are the bright tourist towns of Ventimiglia and Bordighera. San Remo (with its famous casino) is the largest resort. East from Genoa, you will find the resort of Nervi with beautiful parks. Further down the coast are the resort towns of Camogli, Rapallo, Santa Margherita and of course, perhaps the best known and most beautiful Italian port of Portofino. One drawback is the gridlock in and out of Portofino in high season. Sestri Levante makes a good base for exploring the highlight of any trip to Liguria, the Cinque Terre, five beautiful towns, which until recently were accessible only by train or a series of hiking paths. Perched on dramatic cliffs above the sea, you will experience car-free serenity and an Italy of old. Down the coast is Lerici (where we had one of our most memorable meals in an open-air restaurant on the port).

Seafood is dominant in Liguria, especially *branzino* (sea bass), *aragosta* (lobster), *vongole* (clams), *zuppa di datteri* (fish soup), *stoccafisso* (dried cod), *ciuppin* (fish and vegetable stew) and *fritto misto di frutti di mare* (mixed seafood, usually grilled).

Sadly, seafood is becoming less common because of pollution and overfishing in the Mediterranean. *Basilico* (basil) grown in the hills above the sea forms the basis of *pesto* and is common in the cuisine of Liguria. Try *ravioli di magro* (pasta stuffed with herbs and *ricotta* cheese).

LOMBARDY (Milan & the Lake District)

Fashionable, modern Milan is an important center of Italian commerce. If you like to shop, Milan is the place. Tourists often visit four important sites: the Duomo (cathedral, especially the ornate roof), La Scala (the opera house), the Last Supper (at the church of Santa Maria delle Grazie), and the Galleria Vittorio Emanuele (the famous glass-domed shopping center).

In great contrast to Milan is the Lake District, including Lakes Orta (often, regrettably, ignored), Maggiore, Como, and Garda. The towns that line these lakes remain dotted with former palaces (many now resorts) with impressive formal gardens. Many believe the Lake District is Italy at its best. On Lake Como, Bellagio is the most famous resort, but Varenna, with its tiny harbor and splendid beach, is the favorite of many.

Trota (trout) is popular in the Lake District. Lombardy specialties include *stracotto* (pot roast), *ossobuco* (braised veal shank) and *capretto* (roast kid). You will find many dishes served *alla milanese* (battered with eggs and breadcrumbs and fried). *Risotto alla milanese* is a popular rice dish made golden from the ingredient saffron. *Gorgonzola* (a delicious blue cheese) is often found in pasta dishes. Lombardy cheeses also included *crescenza* (a soft, buttery cheese) and *mascarpone* (a very creamy cheese). *Torrone* (honey-and-almond nougat) is a common dessert.

PIEDMONT & VALLE D'AOSTA (Turin & the Alps)

Sometimes the Alpine regions of Piedmont (which means "foot of the mountain") and Valle d'Aosta (north of Piedmont) feel more like France or Switzerland than Italy. Valle d'Aosta has two official languages: Italian and French. Many come to the largest city in these regions, Turin (Torino), to see the Shroud of Turin (believed by some to be the cloth in which Christ's body was wrapped after the crucifixion). North of Turin, into Valle d'Aosta, is Saint Vincent (a popular gambling resort). Any trip to this area would not be complete without a visit to Breuil-Cervina at the base of the Matterhorn (Monte Cervino) with breathtaking views of this famous mountain peak. Courmayeur, another Alpine resort, is the gateway to Mont Blanc (Monte Bianco) on the French border. The walled city of Aosta is nestled in the Alps. Asti (yes, as in the wine), Novara, Vercelli, and Casale Monferrato are all towns with impressive medieval towers. If you're looking for beautiful mountain scenery, don't miss these regions.

Piemontese on a menu means "Piedmont style" or with white truffles. *Tartufi bianchi* are famous white truffles from Alba and Asti. *Alla Valdostana* on a menu means "Valle d'Aosta style" and usually means with ham and cheese. Roast game, sausages and butter play heavy roles in the local diet. *Tajarin* is thin ribbon pasta made golden with egg yolks. *Fonduta* (fondue) is popular. The French influence can be found in *crespelle* (crêpes). You will find *cervo* (venison), *carbonade* (beef cooked in wine and onions) and *arrosto misto* (grilled meats) here along with *trota* (trout). *Gianduiotti* are hazelnut chocolates found in Turin and one of our favorite treats. *Torta di nocciole*, hazelnut cake, is a must.

SAN MARINO (Europe's Oldest Country)

With about only 25,000 people and 24 square miles, San Marino (totally surrounded by Italy) claims to be Europe's oldest existing country. San Marino's official name is the Most Serene Republic of San Marino, and is located 15 miles inland from the Adriatic Sea resort of Rimini. Its chief industries are tourism and the sale of postage stamps. Mt. Titano, upon which San Marino sits, must be climbed after you leave your car. There are three medieval fortresses on the mountain. The capital, also named San Marino, is a maze of attractive narrow streets.

Food is typical Italian. You'll find *coniglio* (rabbit) and *nidi di rondine* (pasta rolls). Don't miss *caciatella* (San Marino's version of crème caramel).

SARDINIA (SARDEGNA)

The island of Sardinia is located about 115 miles off the western coast of Italy in the Mediterranean. Ten miles to the north is the French island of Corsica. Sardinia has been a part of Italy since 1861. Cagliari, the capital, is on the south coast, which is known for its ancient ruins. For the most part, Sardinia remains unspoiled from its rocky coast to its mountainous interior. The northeastern Costa Smeralda (Emerald Coast) is the only area where tourist development has arrived. Those looking for peace and quiet and even isolation should experience the mountainous inland region of Barbagia.

Lobster (*aragosta*) is plentiful along the coast, and the northern coast of Sardinia is sometimes referred to as the lobster coast. Lamb (*agnello*), rabbit (*cunillu*) and trout (*trota*) are ubiquitous. Grilled meats are a specialty. The shepherds of Sardinia feast on *pane carasau*, which is also known as *carta da musica* (music paper). Durham wheat, salt, water and yeast are the simple ingredients for this wood fire-baked bread. You will find this thin, crispy bread used as a pizza crust.

Other specialties of Sardinia include *porceddu* (roast suckling pig which is the "national" dish of Sardinia), *cascà* (couscous), and many honey-based desserts such as *sebadas* (deep-fried cheese-filled ravioli soaked in honey).

SICILY (SICILIA)

F rench, Arabs, Spanish and Italians have all controlled Sicily, the largest and most populated island in the Mediterranean. Travelers will find some of the best-preserved Greek and Roman ruins here, along with the ornate architecture of its churches and palaces. Agrigento is home to the most important archaeological site in Sicily, the Greek "Valley of the Temples." Siracusa (Syracuse) is also known for its Greek and Roman ruins. The capital is Palermo, but most travelers head to the medieval town of Taormina on the east coast in the shadows of Mount Etna, an active volcano. Messina (destroyed by both an earthquake and the bombs of World War II) has bland, modern architecture, and is in strong contrast to the picturesque fishing port of Cefalù.

Sicilian cuisine is not simply pasta and olive oil but incorporates Italian, Greek, French, Spanish and Arab influences. Some specialties are *pasta con le sarde* (pasta with fresh sardines), *pesce spada* (swordfish), and the simple *cicina* (a mixture of fried small fish).

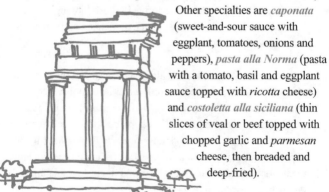

Other specialties are *caponata* (sweet-and-sour sauce with eggplant, tomatoes, onions and peppers), *pasta alla Norma* (pasta with a tomato, basil and eggplant sauce topped with *ricotta* cheese) and *costoletta alla siciliana* (thin slices of veal or beef topped with chopped garlic and *parmesan* cheese, then breaded and deep-fried).

Desserts, and Sicilians

are famous for their desserts, include *cannoli* (pastry tubes filled with sweetened *ricotta* cheese) and *cassata alla siciliana* (layered spongecake).

Marsala wine (from the town of the same name) is a fortified wine that can range from rich and sweet to dry.

TICINO (Italian-Speaking Switzerland)

Ticino is the main Italian-speaking canton or region of Switzerland. Palm trees, Italian architecture, Swiss orderliness and Italian food all make Ticino (with its famous resorts of Lugano and Locarno) a great travel destination. Ticino is Switzerland's southernmost canton, bordering on Italy, and has been a part of Switzerland since the early 1800s. This region has always remained strongly Italian. Italian is one of four official languages of Switzerland (along with French, German and Romansh).

Specialties found in Ticino are *risotto ai fiori di zucca* (a rice dish made with a heavy cream base and zucchini flowers stirred in along with *parmesan* cheese), *pancetta arrotolata* (rolled bacon flavored with cloves), *capretto* (baby goat), *fritto misto* (breaded and fried lake fish), *cotto antico* (bay leaf-flavored salami), and *giambonetti di pollo* (stuffed chicken leg). Bread is a staple in all meals, especially bread with a thick crust dusted with flour called *crusca*. Two common cheeses found in Ticino are *formaggini di capra* (fresh goat's-milk cheese) and *formaggini d'Alpe* (a common cow's-milk cheese). Both of these cheeses are eaten with olive oil, salt and pepper.

TRENTINO-ALTO ADIGE (The Dolomites)

The Alto Adige is the far north of Italy and is more like Austria than Italy. The Dolomite Mountains dominate this area. At the Brenner Pass, on the border with Austria, is the town of Bolzano/Bozen (Austrian until 1918). Near Bolzano is the wine town of Caldaro. Bressanone/Brixen is a beautiful mountain town and the Alto Adige's oldest city. Ortisei, San Martino and Madonna di Campiglio are all summer and winter resort towns. Breathtaking views abound in Brunico/Bruneck. Merano has an interesting old town and famous spas. Trento, the capital of Trentino, is more Italian than Austrian and remains an attractive and architecturally interesting town.

Food here is more German than Italian (especially the farther north you travel). Game, dumplings (*knoedel*) and cured ham (*speck*) all stress the German influence. Sauerkraut (*crauti*) is featured heavily in dishes, as are *wurstel* (hot dogs and brats). For dessert, apples, grown in large numbers in the region, are often added to the Germanic dessert of *strudel*.

TUSCANY (One of the World's Most Popular Destinations)

There are so many picturesque towns in Tuscany, space allows only a few highlights. With unspoiled hills, perfectly preserved towns and great food and wine, Tuscany is one of the most popular tourist destinations in Italy and the world. Since child-hood, we wanted to see the Leaning Tower of Pisa (and the nearby and lesser-known baptistery). There's so much more to this vibrant and interesting city than just the tower. Siena's main square, the Piazza del Campo, and ornate cathedral are only two gems in the beautiful town with (thankfully) a car-free cen-ter. San Gimignano, with its walls and towers, is an incredibly picturesque town. The hilltop towns of Lucca, Montepulciano, Montalcino and Pienza are all worth a visit. Of course, Florence is the favorite of many visitors to Italy. Its wealth of art, housed in buildings which themselves are art, leaves many visitors want-ing to return again and again.

Start your meal with *crostini* (toasted bread with various top-pings). *La bistecca alla Fiorentina*, a T-bone steak, must not be missed, nor should any of the *pecorino* cheeses. Menus often include dishes served *alla lepre* (in a rabbit-based sauce), *cinghiale* (wild boar), *arista* (roast, seasoned pork loin), and *ribollita* (bean and/or cabbage soup which means "twice-cooked soup). *Chianti*, *chianti* and more *chianti*. Enough said!

UMBRIA (Assisi & the Hill Towns North of Rome)

Green hills, towns spared from industrialization, and wonderful dining combine to make Umbria an outstanding Italian destination (especially by car). Perugia is Umbria's largest city with a historic city center, but most tourists come here to visit the smaller towns like Gubbio in northern Umbria. Orvieto is located on a monumental square-shaped rock visible for miles. Don't miss this impressive and well-preserved town (or a taste of its famous wines). Assisi is home to a huge basilica built in memory of local hero St. Francis. It's ironic that such a huge basilica was built for such a humble man, or that the streets are filled with shops selling St. Francis keychains. Still, Assisi, perched on a hill, is a memorable sight. Walled Spoleto (home of the well-known art festival) is dominated by a large castle and is surrounded by wooded countryside.

Tartufi (truffles) are a specialty here, especially the black truffle (*tartufo nero*). *Stringozzi* (homemade pasta) is used in many dishes, especially in Spoleto. *Strozzapreti* (dumplings with meat sauce) is a dish with the strange name of "priest stranglers" after a priest allegedly choked on it. *Palombacci* are small songbirds cooked whole on a spit. For dessert, try *stinchetti* (marzipan cakes). Of course, no one thinks of eating in Umbria without drinking one of the many fine wines of this region.

VENETO (Venice & its Environs)

Veneto is the region around Venice. Despite the tourists, the sometimes smelly canals and the often

inflated prices, Venice is unlike anywhere else in the world. Many cities claim to be pedestrian only, but Venice is truly car-free. Don't just take a day trip here. Once the day trippers leave, Venice becomes a quiet, romantic maze of streets with spectacular architecture. As many times as we have visited, we are always amazed at the splendid beauty of Venice with its buildings rising out of the sea. Don't miss the Piazza San Marco, the Bridge of Sighs, the Basilica di San Marco and the Doge's Palace. If time permits, visit the islands of Murano (famous for its ornate glass), Burano (famous for its lace), San Michele (Venice's island cemetery) and Torcello (for a taste of an almost deserted island).

Veneto includes the cities of Vicenza, Padua (where you can see the "uncorrupted" tongue of St. Anthony), Verona and Treviso. Many towns remain unspoiled and rarely visited by tourists, including Valpolicella (home of this popular Italian red wine), the hills of Colli Euganei (home of hot thermal springs), and Asolo. North of Treviso are the mountain resorts of Cortina d' Ampezzo and Belluno.

Cape sante (scallops), *baccalà* (dried cod), *fegato alla veneziana* (liver with onions), *seppie* (cuttle-fish), and *granseola* (crab) are all specialties of Venice. *Polenta* (the famous cornmeal mush) is found throughout the region. *Carpaccio* is thinly sliced raw beef served in a sauce, and was named by the owner of Harry's Bar in Venice after a famous Venetian painter. *Prosecco* is a slightly sparkling wine from Veneto and worth a try. While in Venice, don't miss having an evening drink or *caffè* in the Piazza San Marco.

This is a brief listing of some familiar English food and food-related words that you may need in a restaurant, followed by a list of phrases that may come in handy.

anchovy, acciuga (acciughe)
appetizer, antipasto (i)
apple, mela (e)
artichoke, carciofo (i)
ashtray, portacenere
asparagus, asparago (i)
bacon, pancetta
baked, al forno
banana, banana (e)
bean, fagiolo (i)
beef, manzo (di bue)
beefsteak, bistecca (di manzo)
beer, birra (e)
beverage, bevanda (e)
bill, conto (i)
bitter, amaro (a)
boiled, bollito/lesso
bottle, bottiglia
bowl, scodella
bread, pane
bread rolls, panino (i)
breakfast, prima colazione
broiled, graticola/griglia
broth, brodo
butter, burro
cabbage, cavolo (i)
cake, torta (e)
candle, candela
carrot, carota (e)
cereal, cereale (i)
chair, sedia

Words that end in A or O are singular

Words that end in E or I are plural

Carciofo ~ Car CHEE OH Foe

bottiglia ~ bow·tee·Lee-ah

Words and letters in parentheses indicate plurals.

Cereale ~ cheer·ee·ah·LaY

check, conto (i)
cheers, salute/cin cin
cheese, formaggio (formaggi)
cherry, ciliegia (e)
chicken soup, brodo di pollo/zuppa di pollo
chicken, pollo
chop, costoletta (e)
clam, vongola (e)
cocktail, cocktail
cod, baccalà/merluzzo
coffee, caffè (also black coffee)
**coffee w/hot water
    (to dilute),** caffè amercano
coffee w/milk, caffè latte
coffee (decaf), caffè hag/caffè decaffeinato
coffee w/cream, caffè con panna
cold, freddo (a)
corn, mais
cover charge, pane coperto
cucumber, cetriolo (i)
cup, coppa
    tazza coffee/tea cup
custard, crema
dessert, dolce (i)
dinner, cena
dish (plate), piatto
drink, bevanda (e)
dry (as in wine), secco
duck, anitra/anatra
egg, uovo (a)
espresso, caffè espresso
fish, pesce
fish soup, zuppa di pesce
fork, forchetta
french fries, patate fritte
fresh, fresco (a)
fried, fritto (a)/fritti (e)

caffè italiano.

caffè americano.

*freddo ~
FRAY-doh*

*dolce ~
dole-chay*

*cena ~
chain-ah*

forchetta.

*forchetta~
FOR-KAY-TAH*

fruit, frutta
game, cacciagione/selvaggina
garlic, aglio
gin, gin
glass, bicchiere
grapefruit, pompelmo
grape, uva
green bean, fagiolino (i)
grilled, griglia or alla griglia
half, mezzo (a)
ham (cooked), prosciutto cotto
ham (cured), prosciutto crudo
hamburger, hamburger
honey, miele
hors d'oeuvre, antipasto
hot, caldo (a)
iced, ghiacciato
ice coffee, caffè freddo
ice cream, gelato (i)
ice (on the rocks), ghiaccio or con ghiaccio
ice water, acqua fredda
iced tea, tè freddo
ketchup, ketchup/salsa di pomodoro
knife, coltello
lamb, abbacchio/agnello
large, grande
lemon, limone (i)
lettuce, lattuga
little (a little), un pó
liver, fegato (fegatini)
lobster, aragosta (e)
loin, lombata
lunch, pranzo
marinated, marinato (a)
match, fiammifero (i)
meat, carne
medium (cooked), a puntino or normale

Bicchiere.
BEE·KEE·AY·RAY

griglia
GREE-LEE·AH

ghiacciato ~
ghee-AH-chee-A·Toe

coltello.

melon, melone
menu, carta or menù
milk, latte
mineral water, acqua minerale
mineral water (sparkling), acqua minerale gasata
mineral water (w/out carbonation), acqua minerale non gasata
mixed, mista (o)
mushroom, fungo (i)
mussel, cozza (e)
mustard, senape
napkin, tovagliolo
noodles, taglierini/pasta
octopus, polipo/polpo
oil, olio
olive oil, olio d'oliva
omelette, frittata
on the rocks (w/ ice), con ghiaccio
onion, cipolla (e)
orange, arancia (arance)
orange juice, succo d'arancia
overdone, ben cotto
oyster, ostrica (ostriche)
pastries, dolci/paste
peach, pesca (pesche)
pear, pera (e)
pea, pisello (i)
pepper (black), pepe
pepper (bell), peperone (i)
perch, pesce persico
pineapple, ananas
plate (dish), piatto
please, per piacere
plum, susina (e)
poached, affogato
pork, maiale

funghi.

Tovagliolo ~
Toe·vah·Lee·oh·Lo

cipolla ~
chee·polla

per piacere ~
pare-pee·ah·chair·AY

maiale ~
my·AL·LAY

potato, patata (e)
poultry, pollame
prawn, gamberetto (i)
rabbit, coniglio
rare, al sangue
raspberry, lampone (i)
receipt, ricevuta/scontrino
rice, riso
roast, arrosto
salad, insalata
salt, sale
sandwich, sandwich/panino (i)
sauce, salsa
saucer, piattino/sottocoppa
sautéed, saltato (i)/saltata (e)
scallops, cappe sante
scrambled, strapazzate
seafood, frutti di mare
seasoning, condimento (i)
shrimp, scampo (i),
    gamberetto (i)
small, piccolo (i)/piccola (e)
smoked, affumicata (o)
snail, lumaca (lumache)
sole, sogliola (e)
soup, zuppa (e)/minestra (e)
spaghetti, spaghetti
sparkling wine, spumante
specialty, specialità
spinach, spinaci
spoon, cucchiaio
squid, calamaro (i)
steak, bistecca
steamed, a vapore
stewed, in umido
strawberry, fragola (e)
sugar, zucchero

Coniglio.
Co-NEE-LEO

ricevuta ~
ree-chay-voo-tah

gamberetto.

Lumaca.

spaghetti ~
spa-get-tee

cucchiaio ~
KOO KEE AYE OH

Zucchero ~
ZOO-KARE-

sugar substitute, dolcificante
supper, cena
sweet, dolce   *dolce* – DOL-CHAY
table, tavolo
tea, tè
tea w/lemon, tè al limone
tea w/milk, tè al latte   TAZZA di tè.
teaspoon, cucchiaino
thank you, grazie
tip, mancia
toasted, tostato
tomato, pomodoro (i)
trout, trota
tumbler (glass), bicchiere
tuna, tonno
turkey, tacchino   *tacchino*
utensil, posata (e)/utensile (i)   TA-KEE-NO
veal, vitello
veal scallop, scaloppa di vitello
vegetable, legume (i). *Verdura (e)* green vegetables
vegetarian, vegetariana (o)
venison, carne di cervo
vinegar, aceto
waiter, cameriere
waitress, cameriera
water, acqua
well done, ben cotto
whipped cream, panna montata
wine, vino
wine (full-bodied), vino corposo
wine list, lista dei vini
wine (red), vino rosso
wine (rosé), vino rosé
wine (white), vino bianco

Unless there's a written translation, it pretty much sounds like it looks, only more Italian sounding. Don't forget to pronounce that final 'E'!

Helpful Phrases

Prego (*preh-go*) can mean: thank you, you're welcome, this way (with a hand gesture), please, okay, and can I help you.
Ciao means hello *and* goodbye. *chow*
Italians answer the phone with ***Pronto?*** *prohn-toh*

please, per favore *pehr-fah-voh-ray*
thank you, grazie *graht-see-ay*
yes, sì *see*
no, no *noh*
good morning, buon giorno *bwohn-jor-noh*
good afternoon/evening, buona sera *bwohn-ah- say-rah*
good night, buona notte *bwohn-ah noht-tay*
goodbye, arrivederci *ah-ree-veh-dehr-chee*
do you speak English?, parla inglese? *par-lah een-gleh-zay*
I don't speak Italian, non parlo l'italiano *nohn par-loh*
    lee-tah-lee-ah-noh

excuse me, mi scusi (or *scusi*) *mee-skoo-zee*
I don't understand, non capisco *nohn kah-pees-koh*
waiter, cameriere *kah-meh-ree-eh-ray*
waitress, cameriera *kah-meh-ree-eh-rah*
I'd like..., Vorrei... *voh-reh-ee*
I'd like a table, Vorrei un tavolo *voh-reh-ee oon-tah-voh-loh*
I'd like to make a reservation, Vorrei prenotare *voh-reh-ee*
    preh-noh-tah-ray

for one person, per uno (una) *OONO*
for two, per due (2), tre (3), quattro (4), cinque (5), *DOO AY*
sei (6), sette (7), otto (8), nove (9), dieci (10) *TRAY / KWATRO / CHINK·WAY*
today/tomorrow, oggi *oh-jee*/domani *doh-mah-nee* *SAY / SET·TAY / OH TOE / NO VAY / dee AY CHI*
by the window, vicino alla finestra *vee-chee-noh*
    ah-lah fee-neh-strah

outside, fuori *fwoh-ree*/**inside,** dentro *dehn-troh*
where is?, dov'è *doh-vey*
the bathroom, il bagno/la toilette *eel bahn-nyoh/lah twah-leh-tay*
the bill, il conto *eel kohn-toh*
service (not) included, servizio (non) incluso *sehr-veet-see-oh*
    (nohn) een-kloo-zoh

a mistake, errore *eh-roh-ray*

credit card, carta di credito *kar-tah dee kreh-dee-toh*

how much does this cost?, quanto costa? *kwahn-toh koh-stah*

what is this?, cos' è questo? *koh-zeh kweh-stoh*

I did not order this, Io questo non l'ho ordinato *ee-oh kweh-stoh nohn loh or-dee-nah-toh*

this is, questo è *kweh-stoh eh*

a little, un po' *oon poh*

hot, caldo (a) *kahl-do*/**cold,** freddo (a) *freh-doh*

spicy (hot), piccante *pee-kahn-tay*

vegetarian, vegetariano/a *soh-noh veh-jeh-tah-ryah-noh/ah*

I don't eat,... Non mangio *nohn mahn-joh*

allergic, allergico (a) *ah-lehr-jee-koh*

dairy, latticini *lah-tee-chee-nee*

wheat/gluten, frumento *froo-mehn-toh*/glutine *gloo-tee-nay*

seafood, frutti di mare *froo-tee dee mah-ray*

shellfish, molluschi e crostacei *moh-loo-skee ay kroh-stah-cheh-ee*

nuts, noci e altra frutta secca *noh-chee ay ahl-trah froo-tah seh-kah*

peanuts, arachidi *ah-rah-kee-dee*

diabetic, diabete *dee-ah-beh-tay*

kosher, kasher *kah-shehr*

no caffeine, senza caffeina *sehnt-sah kah-feh-ee-nah*

no alcohol, niente alcool *nee-ehn-tay ahl-kohl*

vegetarian, vegetariano (a) *veh-jeh-tah-ree-ah-noh*

vegan, vegano (a) *veh-gah-noh*

undercooked, troppo crudo *troh-poh kroo-doh*

overcooked, troppo cotto *troh-poh koh-toh*

delicious, delizioso (a) *deh-leet-see-oh-zoh*

light (low-fat), leggero *leh-jeh-roh*

open, aperto *ah-pehr-toh*/**closed,** chiuso *kee-oo-zoh*

Monday, lunedì *loo-nay-dee*

Tuesday, martedì *mart-ay-dee*

Wednesday, mercoledì *mehr-cohl-ay-dee*

Thursday, giovedì *joh-vay-dee*

Friday, venerdì *ven-nehr-dee*

Saturday, sabato *sah-bah-toh*

Sunday, domenica *doh-mehn-nee-kah*

abbacchio, lamb

abbacchio alla cacciatora, pieces of lamb braised w/rosemary,
   garlic, wine & peppers

abbacchio alla romana, pieces of lamb cooked until brown,
   then roasted in a rosemary, garlic, vinegar & anchovy sauce

abbacchio brodettato, pieces of lamb cooked in a broth of
   lemon, parsley & beaten eggs

abboccatto, a medium-sweet wine

abbrustolito, toasted

abruzzese, red pepper sauce

acciuga (acciughe), anchovy

acciughe al limone, anchovies w/lemon-based sauce

acerbo, sour

aceto, vinegar

aceto balsamico, balsamic vinegar. Aged vinegar
   used in many dishes, especially salads

acetosella, sorrel

acido, sour

acini di pepe, pasta for soup in the shape of peppercorns

acqua, water

acqua brillante, tonic water

acquacotta, bread & vegetable soup

acquadella, small whitebait fish

acqua di rubinetto, tap water

acqua di seltz, seltzer water/soda water

acqua fredda, ice water

acqua gasata, carbonated water

acqua ghiacciata, ice water

acqua minerale, mineral water

acqua minerale frizzante, extremely carbonated water

acqua minerale naturale, mineral water w/out carbonation

acqua naturale, tap water

acqua non gasata, water w/out carbonation

acqua non potabile, do not drink the water!

acqua pazza, sauce of tomato, garlic, oil, parsley & chili pepper

acqua semplice, tap water

acqua tonica, tonic water

Acquavite, brandy/distilled spirit flavored w/caraway

affettato, sliced

[handwritten note:] acciuga ~ AH·cHEE·oo·ga

[handwritten note:] "Acqua cotta" means cooked water

affettato (i), cold cut

affogato, poached. This can also refer to ice cream soaked in coffee or liqueur

affumicato, smoked

agliata/all'aglio, garlic sauce

aglio, garlic

aglio e olio, w/garlic & olive oil

aglione, mixture of garlic, sea salt, rosemary & sage

Aglio.

agnello, lamb

agnello alla turca, lamb stew w/raisins

agnello con salsa di uovo, lamb w/egg sauce.

agnolotti, filled pasta (square shaped)

agone, freshwater fish found in the lake country (the size of sardines)

agresto, juice of unripened grapes

agro, lemon juice & olive oil dressing

agrodolce, sweet & sour sauce

ai/al/all'/alla, in the style of/with

Agresto is sometimes used in place of vinegar

ajula, sea bream

ala, wing

alaccia, large sardine

alalunga, albacore (a type of tuna)

Albana, dry to semi-sweet wine from Emilia-Romagna

albicocca (albicocche), apricot

albume, egg white

alcolica, alcoholic. *Una bevanda alcolica* is an alcoholic beverage

alcool, alcol

Aleatico, dessert wine (made from muscat grapes)

alette, wing

alfabetini, alphabet noodles for soup

al forno, baked

alfredo, w/butter & cream sauce

al fresco, outside (in the fresh air)

alice (i), anchovy

allodola (e), lark

alloro, bay leaf

ALLORO.

amabile, slightly sweet wine

amarena (e), sour cherry

amaretti, macaroons

amaretto, sweet almond-flavored liqueur

amaro, bitter/bitter cordial (bitters)

amatriciana, bacon, tomato & spices sauce

amburghese/amburgo, hamburger/ground meat
amburghese alla tirolese, hamburger served w/onion rings
Americano, Campari, vermouth & lemon peel
ammiru, prawns in Sicily
analcolico (i), non-alcoholic
ananas, pineapple
anatra, duck
anatroccolo, duckling
anelli/anellini, small circular
    pasta for soup (ring pasta)
aneto, dill
anguidda, another name for eel in Sicily
anguilla (e), eel
anguilla alla veneziana, eel braised
    w/tuna & lemon sauce
anguria, watermelon
anice, anise
animelle, sweetbreads
animelle alla salvia, sweetbreads w/sage
anisetta, anise-flavored liquor
anitra, duck
anitra germano, mallard duck
anitra selvatica, wild duck
annegati, slices of meat in wine
antipasto (i), appetizer
**antipasto alla marinara/antipasto di mare/antipasto di
    pesce,** assorted seafood
antipasto misto, assorted appetizers
aperitivo, aperitif
arachide (i), peanut
aragosta (e), lobster (crayfish)
arancia (e), orange. *All' arancia* means w/orange juice
aranciata, orangeade/orange soda
arancino (i) di riso, breaded ball of cooked rice stuffed w/meat
& deep-fried. It gets its name from its resemblance to an
orange
argentina, argentine fish
arigusta, crawfish
aringa, herring
aringa affumicata, smoked herring
arista, roast, seasoned pork loin
arista alla fiorentina, roasted pork rubbed w/garlic paste,
    cloves, salt, rosemary, pepper

In Perugia Anguilla can also refer to an eel shaped pastry created originally by nuns.

37

arista di maiale/arista di suino, pork loin

arrabbiata, all', w/a spicy tomato & herb sauce

arrostetti, small roast

arrosti misti freddi, a selection of cold roasted meats

arrostini, veal chops

arrostino, small roast

arrostino annegato, small veal roast
served with mushrooms

arrostite, grilled/roasted

arrosto/arrostito, roast/roasted

arrosto alla genovese, a roast w/onions, mushrooms
& tomatoes

arrosto alla montanara, pot roast

arrosto con pastine, roast w/dough crust

arrosto di manzo, roast beef

arrosto in porchetta, roast suckling pig stuffed w/garlic,
bacon & herbs

arrosto misto, mixed roast meats

arrosto morto, pot roast

arsella (e), mussel

asciutta (o), dry. Also refers to pasta w/sauce
(as opposed to pasta for soup)

asiago, sharp cheese (round-shaped cheese)

asiago dolce, mild *asiago*

asparago (i), asparagus

asparago alla bismark, asparagus w/melted butter & fried egg

asparago alla milanese/asparago all'uovo, asapagus topped
w/melted butter, *parmesan* cheese & fried egg

assortito (i), assorted

astaco/astice, lobster

Asti Spumante, sparkling white wine

attorta, fruit- & almond-filled pastry

Aurum, orange liqueur

avvoltino, standing roast or rolled roast

babà, spongecake covered w/rum

babaluci, snails in tomato & onion sauce

bacca (e), berry

baccalà, salt cod

baccalà alla fiorentina, salt cod floured & fried in oil
& tomato sauce

baccalà alla lucana, salt cod cooked w/peppers

baccalà alla vicentina, salt cod w/onion, parsley, garlic,
anchovies & cinnamon

ASTI.

bacio, chocolate hazelnut (means "kiss")

bagna cauda/bagna caoda, hot vegetable dip w/anchovies

bagnet, sauce (in Piedmont)

balsamella, bechamel/white sauce

banana (e), banana *Good Guess!*

bar, serves espresso, cappuccino, rolls, small sandwiches, alcoholic beverages and soft drinks

barbabietola (e), beet

Barbaresco, soft red wine from Piedmont (lighter & drier than *Barolo*)

Barbera, dry red wine

barbe rosse, beets

Bardolino, pale, light red wine

Andy hates beets even in Italy.

Barolo, rich red wine from Piedmont

basilico, basil

bastoncini, bread sticks (means "little sticks")

battuta scanello, pounded round steak

battutina al prosciutto, hamburger mixed w/cured ham

battuto, finely chopped herbs, onions, celery & carrots

battuto di manzo, ground beef

bavette (i), thin, flat pasta

beccaccia, woodcock

beccaccino, snipe (game)

beccafico, warbler/song bird

belga, Belgian endive

bellini, *Prosecco* & peach juice. Try one at Harry's Bar in Venice

"Bel Paese" means beautiful country

bel paese, smooth, mild & soft cheese

ben cotto, well done

bensone, lemon cake

besciamella, white cream sauce

bevanda (e), drink/beverage

bevanda compresa, cost of drinks included

bianchetti, small anchovy (or sardine)

bianchi, white

bianco, white wine

Bianco di Martina, a fortified wine found in Apulia

bianco, in, w/butter (w/out a sauce)

bibita (e), drink/beverage

bibite analcoliche, soft drinks

bicchiere, glass

Bicchiere.
BEE·KEE·AY·RAY

biete, Swiss chard

bietole, beet/Swiss chard

bietole alla padella, Swiss chard cooked w/butter &/or oil
bietoline, beet greens
bietolini, Swiss chard
bignè/bignole (con crema), cream puff
bigoli, larger form of spaghetti
biova/biovetta, round bread loaf
birra, beer
birra alla spina, tap beer
birra analcolica, no-alcohol beer
birra bionda, light beer
birra chiara, light beer (lager)
birra di barile, draft beer
birra importata, imported beer
birra in bottiglia, bottled beer
birra in lattina, beer in a can
birra scura, dark beer

BiRRA

biscotto (i), cookie/biscuit/cracker/spongecake
biscotti di prato, cookies w/pieces of almond
biscuit tortoni, dessert of beaten egg whites & macaroon crumbs topped w/whipped cream & toasted almonds
bismark, alla, usually means served w/a fried egg
bistecca, steak
bistecca alla bismark, fried steak w/an egg on top
bistecca alla fiorentina, T-bone steak
bistecca alla pizzaiola, steak w/tomato & garlic sauce
bistecca di manzo, beef steak
bistecca di vitello, veal scallop
bistecca Fiorentina, T-bone steak
bistecca impanata, cutlet/chop
bistecche, steaks
bistecchine, thin steaks
bitto, firm, smoked cheese
bobe, sea bream
boccolotti, short tubular pasta
bocconcini, diced veal w/tomato & white wine sauce/*mozzarella* balls
boldro, monkfish in Tuscany
boletus, porcini mushrooms
bollito (i), boiled. Can also mean meat or fish stew
bollito di gallina, boiled chicken
bollito di manzo, boiled beef
bollito misto, mixed boiled meats
bolognese, alla, usually means a tomato & meat sauce

Bistecca Impanata is often breaded and fried in butter

"bocconcini" means mouthful

bomba di riso, rice dish w/ground meat & herb fillings

bombette, pork shoulder stuffed with melted cheese.
A specialty in Apulia

bombolone (i), doughnut

bonèt, chocolate cream dessert. A specialty in Piedmont

borlotti, type of bean

boscaiola, means "woodsman style" & can refer to many
things, including w/wild mushrooms

bosega, mullet

botolo, mullet

bottarga, fish eggs (tuna roe that has been salted & pressed)

bottiglia, bottle

bove, beef

bottiglia~

bovoletti/bovoloni, small snails in Venice

brace, alla, on charcoal

Bow-Tee-Lee AH

braciola (e), rib steak/chop/cutlet

braciola di maiale, pork chop

bracioletta, small slice of meat

bracioletta a scottadito, lamb chops (charcoal grilled)

bracioline/braciolone, meat roll

braciolone alla napoletana, breaded steak, rolled & stewed

branzino, bass. *Branzinotti* is small sea bass

brasato, braised/braised meat w/wine

bresaola, thinly sliced cured raw beef

briciole di pane, breadcrumbs

brioche, buns/rolls/small loaf (used for breakfast)

broccoletti, broccoli

broccoletti di rape, turnip greens

broccoletti strascinati, broccoli sautéed w/garlic & bacon

broccolo (i), broccoli

brodetto, rich fish soup

brodo, broth/soup/bouillon.
In brodo means cooked in broth

brodo di manzo, consomme/beef broth

brodo di pollo, chicken soup

brogue, sea bream

brovada, marinated turnips w/pork sausage

Broccolo.

Brunello, full-bodied red wine from Montalcino

bruschetta, grilled bread w/garlic & olive oil (frequently
topped w/tomatoes &/or onions)

brut, very dry wine

brutti, small almond cakes

bucaniera, tomato & garlic seafood sauce

Bucaniera...
Buccaneer,
get it?

bucatini, hollow spaghetti noodles

bucatoni, same as *bucatini*, but larger

budino, custard/pudding

budino alla toscana, cream cheese w/raisins, almonds, sugar & egg yolks

bue, beef

burrata, a very buttery cheese found in Apulia

burrida, fish stew or casserole. In Sardinia this refers to a poached & marinated fish dish

burrini, a type of hard, aged cheese

burro, butter

burro maggiordomo, butter w/lemon juice & parsley

busecca, tripe & vegetable soup

buttiri, a type of hard, aged cheese

cacao, cocoa

cacasor cioccolata, cocoa

cacciagione, game

cacciatora, alla/cacciatore, w/mushrooms, wine, tomatoes & herbs

cacciucco, spicy fish soup

cachi, persimmons

caciatella, a crème caramel dessert

cacio, *pecorino* cheese

caciocavallo, a hard, aged cheese made of whole milk

cacio e pepe, sauce made of black pepper & *pecorino* cheese

cacio e uova, w/cheese & egg

caciotta, mild cheese

caciucco, fish soup

caffè, coffee

caffè al vetro, coffee served in a glass

caffè americano, American-style coffee (Italian coffee diluted w/hot water)

caffè con panna, coffee w/cream

caffè corretto, *espresso* w/a shot of liquor (usually brandy)

caffè doppio, coffee (a double serving)

caffè espresso, *espresso*

caffè freddo, iced coffee

caffè hag, decaffeinated coffee

caffè latte, coffee w/steamed milk

caffè lungo, coffee w/water (weaker coffee)

alla cacciatora means in the style of the hunter

Traditionally there must be as many types of fish in the soup as C's in cacciucco.

caffè macchiato, coffee w/a small amount of warm milk
caffè nero, black coffee
caffè ristretto, small, thick & strong
    coffee (stronger than an *espresso*)
calamaretto (i), small squid
calamari, squid
calamari fritti, fried squid
calamito, grey mullet
caldo (a)/caldi (e), warm or hot
caldaro, fish & potato soup
calzone (i), folded & stuffed pizza
cameriera, waitress
cameriere, waiter
camicia, in, poached
camomilla, camomile tea
camoscio, small deer (chamois)
campagnola, alla, w/vegetables & herbs
Campari, red aperitif w/a bitter, quinine taste
campo, del, wild. *Cicoria del campo* is wild chicory
candita (o), candied
canederli, dumplings made w/ham, sausage & breadcrumbs
canestrelli, sweet pastry/small sea snail or scallop
cannella, cinnamon
cannellini, small white beans found in Tuscany
cannelloni, large tube pasta stuffed w/fillings
cannelloni al forno, stuffed & browned in oven
cannelloni alla Barbaroux, stuffed w/ham, veal & cheese
cannelloni alla laziale, stuffed w/meat & onions
cannelloni alla napoletana, stuffed w/ham & cheese
    w/tomato & herb sauce
cannelloni alla piemontese, stuffed w/veal, ham & cheese
cannocchie, see *canoce*
cannoli alla siciliana, *ricotta* cheese-filled pastry
    w/sugar glaze
cannolicchio, razor-shell clam
cannolo (i), custard-filled pastry w/candied fruit or sweet
    white cheese (*ricotta*). This
    also refers to a short pasta tube
canoce, Venetian word for
    cannocchie which is neither a
    shrimp nor a lobster but some-
    thing in between
cantarello, chanterelle mushroom

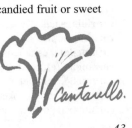

cantucci, almond biscuits

capelli d'angelo, thin noodle soup ("angel hair")

capellini, long, thin, fine spaghetti

capelunghe, razor clams

cape sante, scallops in Venice

capitone, large eel

capocollo, smoked pork salami

caponata, cold dish of eggplant & vegetables.
  Eggplant, celery & onions are fried separately &
  cooked in a sweet & sour sauce of raisins, tomatoes,
  pine nuts, sugar & vinegar

caponata di melanzane, eggplant & pepper stew

cappelle di funghi, mushroom caps

cappelletti, rings of pasta filled w/ground meat.
  Some think they look like little caps

cappello da prete, a triangular
  sausage ("priest's hat")

cappero (i), caper

cappesante, scallops (means
  "sacred shells")

capponcello ruspante al forno,
  roast farm-raised capon

cappone, capon

cappon magro, vegetables & fish stacked high on a plate

cappuccino, coffee w/steamed milk

capra, goat

caprese, *mozzarella* & tomatoes. **Pasta caprese** is pasta
  w/tomatoes, *mozzarella* & basil. *Caprese* means
  from the island of Capri

capretto, baby goat

capretto al forno, roasted kid stuffed w/herbs

capretto alla pasqualina, roasted baby goat (an Easter dish)

capricciosa (o), chef's special (means "caprice" or "whim")

caprino, mild goat's-milk cheese

caprino fresco, a fresh goat's-milk cheese

caprino romano, hard goat's-milk cheese

capriolo, small deer (roebuck)

caraffa, carafe

caramellate, caramelized

caramella (e), candy (not chocolate)

caramello, caramel

carbonade, beef cooked in wine & onions

carbonara, pasta w/bacon (or ham), cheese, olive oil & eggs

"Cappello da prete" means "priest's hat."

carbonata, grilled pork chop. Sometimes this
refers to beef stew in red wine

carciofi alla giudea, deep-fried artichokes
(prepared in the shape of a rose).
This term means "Jewish-style artichokes"

carciofi alla romana, artichokes stuffed w/garlic, parsley &
mint, cooked in olive oil & white wine

carciofi in pinzimonio, raw artichokes in an oil dressing

carciofini in umido, artichole hearts sautéed in garlic & tomatoes

carciofini sott'olio, artichokes in olive oil

carciofino (i), small artichoke

carciofo (i), artichoke. The bottoms of artichokes are the *fondi
di carciofi*

cardo (i), cardoon, a vegetable that looks like celery
but tastes like artichokes

carne, meat

carne a carrargiu, spit-roasted meat

carne cruda all`albese, slices of raw steak

carne di cervo, venison

carne macinata, ground meat

carne per arrosto in pentola, pot roast

carne tritata, ground meat

carone, large white beans

carota (e), carrot

carpa/carpione, carp

carpaccio, thinly sliced raw beef w/sauce. Named by the owner
of Harry's Bar in Venice after a famous Venetian painter

carpaccio di branzino, slices of raw sea bass w/a sauce

carpione, in, served cold w/vinegar sauce

carrargiu, spit-roasted

carré, sliced bread ("square")

carrè di..., roast loin of... *Carrè di agnello* is rack of lamb

carrello, al, served from the food cart

carrettiera, tuna, garlic & pork sauce

carruba, carob

carta, menu

carta da musica, flat, crispy bread of Sardinia. See *pane carasau*

carteddate/cartellate, fried pastry dipped in honey

cartoccio, al, roasted (often in a paper bag, foil or other
covering). The covering is opened at the table

carvi (grani di), caraway (seeds)

casa, house. *Della casa* means "house specialty"

carciofo.

"Carré" means square.

casalinga (o), homemade

cascà, the Sardinian version of couscous

casoncelli, pasta stuffed w/ground meat

cassata, ice cream (or sweet *ricotta* cheese) w/candied fruit

cassata alla siciliana, *ricotta* cheese-filled layered cake w/sugar glaze

cassata gelata, various flavors of ice cream w/candied fruit

casserola/casseruola, casserole

cassoela/cassoeula, pork casserole

castagna (e), chestnut

castagnaccio, chestnut cake

castagnole, chestnut fritters

castellana, stuffed veal cutlet

Castelli Romani, white table wine from the area southeast of Rome

Cavoletti.

castrato, mutton

catalogna, a type of salad green (like spinach, often cooked)

cauladda, Sardinian soup of cabbage, beans, sausage & meats

cavalla, mackerel. Also refers to a female horse

cavatappi, tubular pasta in the shape of a corkscrew

cavatelli/cavatieddi, homemade pasta

caviale, caviar

caviale del sud, "caviar of the south." Calabrian dish of dried small fish preserved in oil & powdered w/*peperoncino*

cavoletti, Brussels sprouts

cavolfiore, cauliflower

cavolini di Bruxelles/cavoli di Brusselle, Brussels sprouts

cavolo (i), cabbage

cavolo broccoluto, broccoli

cavolo riccio, kale

cavolo rosso, red cabbage

cavolo verde, green cabbage

cazzoeula, pork casserole

cecatelli, homemade pasta

cece (i), chickpea/garbanzo

ceche, baby eels

ceci alla Pisana, chickpea stew

cedrata/cedro, a large fruit that resembles a lemon. The peel is used for flavoring

cee alla Pisana, baby-eel dish from Pisa

cefalo, grey mullet

cena, dinner

EELS BREED in fresh water & mature in the sea.

Cena – Chain-ah

cenci, fried pastry

Centerbe, green herb liqueur

cèpes, porcini mushroom

Cerasella, cherry liqueur

cereale, cereal

cerfoglio, chervil

cernia, grouper

Certosino, green or yellow herb liqueur.
This is also the name for a soft & mild cheese

cervella, brains

cervo, venison

cestino di frutta, a basket of fruit

cetriolino (i), pickle

cetriolo (i), cucumber

cevapcici, grilled meatballs found near Italian/Slovenian border

charlotte, spongecake & whipped-cream dessert

Chianti, well-known medium-bodied red wine from Tuscany.
Chianti Classico comes from the center of the Chianti region, is aged for at least one year & is more complex.
Riserva denotes a *Chianti* aged for at least two years

chiare, egg whites

Chiaretto, young & popular rosé wine

chicche, small potato *gnocchi*

chifferi, "c"-shaped tubular pasta

chiocciola (e), snail/sea shell-shaped pasta

chiocciolina, little snail

chiocciolini, spiral-shaped buns

chiodi di garofani, cloves

chiodino (i) a type of mushroom

chiodo di garofano, clove

ciabatta, large, coarse bread loaf

ciauscolo, soft, fatty pork sausage

cialda (e), waffle/wafer

cialledda, vegetable soup w/bread, olives, tomato, hard-boiled eggs & olive oil. A specialty in Basilicata

cialsons/chialzons, sweet & sour pasta

ciambella/chiambella/ciambelline, donut (not fried like North American donuts)

cibo, food

cibreo, chicken-liver dish

cicale di mare, type of shrimp (this crustacean is found off the coast of Italy. The name means "grasshopper")

cicchetti/cicheti, snacks served in Venice. Similar to *tapas*

cicina, mixture of small fried fish

cicoria, chicory/endive

ciliegia (e), cherry

cima, stuffed veal served cold

cima alla genovese, veal stuffed w/mushrooms & sausage

cimalino, *cima* served w/beans. **Cimalino di manzo** is stuffed breast of beef

cime di rape, turnip greens

cinese, Chinese

cinghiale, wild boar

Cinque Terre, a dry, light white wine from the spectacularly beautiful five towns on the western coast of Italy

cioccolata, chocolate

cioccolata calda, hot chocolate

cioccolato, chocolate (hot chocolate)

ciociara, a seasoned meat sauce

cioppino, fish stew (this word is usually used only in the United States)

cipolla (e), onion

cipollina (e), chive

cipolline novelle, green onions

cipollotti, spring onions

ciriola, small eel

ciuppin, thick fish (& vegetable) soup

civraxin, Sardinian large bread loaf

cocco/noce di cocco, coconut

cocktail di vongole, clam cocktail (clams, olive oil & lemon)

cocomero, watermelon

cocozelle, zucchini

coda, tail

coda alla vaccinara, oxtail stew in a tomato & garlic sauce

Cocomero.

coda di bue, oxtail

coda di rospo, monkfish

coglioni di mulo, finely ground pork sausage threaded with a wide strip of lard. The name means "mule's balls"

cognac, cognac

colazione (prima), breakfast

collo, neck

colomba, dove-shaped cake. **Colombo** means pigeon

colombacchi, wild pigeon

coltello, knife

composta, stewed fruit (compote)

composta cotta, mixed cold, cooked vegetables

con, with

conchiglie, shell-shaped pasta. *Conchigliette* is a small version used in soup

condimento (i), condiment

confetti, sugared almonds (used in weddings & special occasions)

confettura, jam

con ghiaccio, on the rocks

coniglio, rabbit

coniglio all'agro, rabbit stewed in red wine

coniglio all'Anconetana, a stuffed-rabbit dish

cono, cone (as in ice cream cone)

con seltz, w/soda

conserva, preserves/jam/jelly

conserva di frutta, preserves/jam/jelly

consommè, consomme (clear soup)

consommè madrilena, clear tomato soup

consommè reale, chicken consomme

Coniglio.
CO-NEE-LEO

contadina, alla, usually means served in a tomato & mushroom sauce (means "peasant woman")

conto, check/bill

contorno (i), side dish/garnish. This often refers to a vegetable side dish

contrafiletto/controfiletto, sirloin

copata, honey & nut wafer

coperto, cover charge

coppa, cup/goblet/small bowl. *Coppa* can also refer to smoked ham or smoked bacon

coppa di frutta, fruit cup/fruit cocktail

coppa di gamberetti, shrimp cocktail

coppa gelato, cup of ice cream/sundae

coratella di abbacchio, lamb heart, lung & liver dish

corda, lamb-tripe dish

cordulla, Sardinian dish made w/intestines

coregone, a type of salmon

coriandolo, coriander

cornetti, string beans

cornetto, croissant

corona, large white bean

'Cornetto' means trumpet.

49

corposo, full-bodied wine

corretto, coffee or *espresso*
w/a shot of alcohol

Cortese, dry white wine

Corvo, dry, light white wine from Sicily

cosce di rana, frogs' legs

coscetta, leg/drumstick

coscia, leg

cosciette di rane, frogs' legs

cosciotto, leg

cosciotto di agnello, leg of lamb

cosciotto di porcello, leg of young lamb

costa, rib/scallop

costa di manzo, rib roast/T-bone steak

costa di sedano, celery stalk

costarelle di abbacchio a scottadito, grilled lamb cutlet

costarelli, spareribs/pork chops

costata, chop/beef steak. *Costata di vitello* is a veal chop.
Costata di manzo is rib steak

costata alla fiorentina, grilled beef steak

costata alla pizzaiola, braised beef steak in a tomato sauce &
mozzarella cheese

costate, rib steaks

costate d'agnello, rack of lamb

costatella, rib steak

**costellata/costelleta/
costelletine,** rib steak

costicini, pork spareribs

costine, pork spareribs

costola arrostita, rib roast

costolatura, beef loin

costole di manzo, prime rib

We have found that European cuts of meat often look nothing like cuts of the same name in the States.

costoletta (e), cutlet/chop (often coated in eggs & breadcrumbs
& fried in butter)

costoletta alla bolognese, breaded veal cutlet w/tomato sauce,
cheese & ham

costoletta alla milanese, breaded & fried veal cutlet

costoletta alla parmigiana, cutlet breaded & baked w/
parmesan cheese

costoletta alla siciliana, thin slices of veal or beef topped
w/chopped garlic & *parmesan* cheese, breaded & deep-fried

costoletta alla valdostana, cutlet w/ham & cheese stuffing

costoletta alla viennese, wiener schnitzel
costoletta di vitello impanata, breaded veal cutlet
costolette di tonno, tuna steaks
costolette di vitello, veal chops
costolettine, lamb or pork chop
cotechino/coteghino, spicy pork sausage
cotognata, quince marmalade
cotogne, quince
cotoletta (e), cutlet, usually a veal cutlet
cotoletta alla bolognese, breaded veal cutlet topped w/ham,
   cheese & tomato sauce
cotto, cooked
cotto antico, bay leaf-flavored salami
cotto a puntino, medium done
courgette, zucchini
cozza (e), mussel
cozze alla marinara, mussels in white wine, garlic & parsley
cozze Posillipo, mussels in a spicy tomato sauce
crauti, sauerkraut
crema, cream/custard
crema caramella, custard w/caramelized-sugar topping
crema da montare, whipping cream
crema di, cream of
crema di funghi, cream of mushroom soup
crema di piselli, cream of pea soup
crema di pollo, cream of chicken soup
crema di verdura, puree of vegetables
crema fritta, fried-custard dessert
crema inglese, custard w/stewed fruit or cake
crème caramel, caramel custard
cremini, a type of mushroom
cremino, ice cream bar/a soft cheese
cren, horseradish
crescenza, a soft, buttery cheese (w/relatively low fat content)
crescionda, Umbrian dessert made from amaretto cookies,
   eggs, milk & unsweetened cocoa
crescione/crescione di fonte, watercress
crespelle, crêpes
crespelle alla fiorentina, spinach crêpes
crespolino, meat-filled pancake
croccheta (e), croquette
crocchette di patate, potato croquettes

Courgette is actually a french word found on menus near the french border.

crocchette di riso, deep-fried rice balls w/cheese in the center

crosta, crust (as in a pie crust)

crostaceo (i), shellfish

crostata, open-faced pie

crostata di frutta, fruit pie

crostini/crostoni, bread, fried or toasted in oil & topped w/many ingredients/croutons

crostini alla napoletana, toast w/cheese & anchovies

crostini alla provatura, toasted diced bread w/*provatura* cheese

crostini di mare, shellfish on fried bread

crostini di milza, toast w/veal paté

crostini Fiorentina, toast w/liver paté

crostini in brodo, croutons in broth

crostone di polenta, roasted meat (usually game) served on a round base of *polenta*

crudo, raw

crusca, bran. This also refers to a bread found in Ticino w/ thick crust & dusted w/flour

cubbaita, nougat w/almonds, honey & sesame seeds

cucchiaio, spoon

cuccia, layered dish of slow-roasted meats, tomato sauce & grains. A specialty in Calabria

"cucina" means kitchen and cooking

cucina, cuisine

culaccio, rump meat

culatello, ham cured in white wine

cumino, cumin

cunillu, Sardinian word for rabbit

cuoco, chef

cuore (i), heart

cuore di sedano, celery heart

cuori di carciofi, artichoke hearts

curry, curry

cuscusu di Trapani, couscous

Cynar, after-dinner drink made of artichokes

daino, deer

da portar via, to go

datteri di mare, mussels

dattero (i), date

decaffeinato, decaffeinated

del giorno, of the day

della casa, of the house

"Decaffeinato" is becoming more common but be prepared for a condescending smile.

dente, al, pasta cooked until it's still slightly firm
(means "to the tooth")

dentice, a Mediterranean fish (dentex) similar to sea bream

denti d'elefante, tubular pasta (like *macaroni*)
(means"elephant's tooth")

di, of

diavola/diavolicchio, usually means served w/pepper or chili
peppers. Can also mean a dish cooked over a flame since
the terms mean "devil"

digestivo, after-dinner drink

diavolo-devil

disossata, boned rib steak

di stagione, in season

ditali, small tubular pasta for soup,
often called thimbles. *Ditalini* is the
smaller version of this pasta

diverso, varied

dolce (i), dessert/sweet/pastry. *Dolce* can also mean sweet wine

Dolcetto, fruity, dry red wine from Piedmont

dolci di Taglierini, sweetened noodle (taglierini) cake

dolcificante, artificial sweetener

dorato (a), browned/golden brown

e means and.

Doria, alla, w/cucumbers

dragoncello, tarragon

é with an accent means is.

e, and

eliche, spiral pasta.
Often refered to as propellers

elicoidali, tubular pasta w/straight edges

emmenthal, Swiss cheese

empanata, breaded

entrecìte/entrecote di bue, boneless rib steak

erbazzone, vegetable pie

erbe, herbs

erbette, cooked greens

espresso, *espresso* (strong, small coffee)

espresso doppio, a double serving of *espresso*

espresso macchiato, *espresso* w/a small amount of foamy milk
on top. Compare this to *latte macchiato*

Est Est Est, a dry, semi-sweet white wine

Etna, red & white Sicilian wines

etto, fish dishes are frequently served by the *etto*
(or 100 grams)

fagianella, bustard (bird)

fagiano, pheasant

fagioli al fiasco, slow-cooked Tuscan bean dish served
w/garlic, herbs & olive oil

fagioli alla maruzzara, beans in an oregano & tomato sauce

fagioli all'Uccelloto, white beans in a tomato sauce

fagioli bianchi, white beans

fagioli bianco di Spagna, lima beans

fagioli cannellini, small white beans

fagioli con le cotiche, beans in a tomato sauce w/slices of pork

fagioli cotti al forno, baked beans

fagioli freschi, fresh beans

fagioli lessati al forno, boiled baked beans

fagioli lessi, shelled, boiled beans

fagiolino (i) green bean/French bean

fagioli rampicanti, runner beans

fagioli rossi, red kidney beans

fagioli sgranati, fresh shelled beans

fagioli toscani, cooked white-bean dish

fagioli verdi, green beans

fagiolo (i), bean

fagottini, food wrapped around a filling

Falerno, dry white & red wines

fame, hungry

faraona, guinea fowl

farcito (a), stuffed

farfalle/farfallette, bow-tie or butterfly-shaped pasta

farfalline (i), bow-tie or butterfly-shaped pasta

farina, flour

farinata, baked pancake made from olive oil, chickpea flour,
salt & pepper (eaten as a snack)

farricello, barley

farro, a type of wheat, similar to spelt

farsumagru, veal or beef roll stuffed w/ham,
bacon, cheese, onions & parsley.
A Sardinian specialty

fasolini, scallops

fatto in casa, homemade

fava (e), broad bean. Sometimes called
fave grande or *fave España*

favarella, bean soup

favata, bean, sausage & bacon casserole

fave al Guanciale, broad beans cooked w/bacon & onions

fagioli.

farfalle.

farricello.

fave e cicoria, puréed fava beans, sautéed chicory &
olive oil. A specialty in Apulia

fegà, liver in Venice

fegatelli di maiale, pork liver

fegato (fegatini), liver.
Fegatini di maiale are pork livers;
fegatini di pollo are chicken livers

fegato alla veneziana, liver & onions

fegato di vitello, calf's liver

Fernet, a bitter digestive liqueur

ferri, ai, sliced & grilled (means "on iron")

fesa, leg of veal

fesa in gelatina, roast veal w/aspic jelly

fetta di/fette di, slice of...

fettina, small slice

fettuccine (i), long, flat, thin ribbon noodle

fettuccine Alfredo, thin ribbon noodles w/cream, butter & nutmeg

fettuccine alla Panna, thin ribbon noodles w/cream, butter &
nutmeg

fettuccine in brodo, noodle soup

fettuna, toasted or grilled over an
open fire w/garlic & olive oil

fettura di melacotogne, quince jam

fiamma, alla, flamed

fiammifero (i), match

fianco, flank

fiasco, straw-covered bottle

fichi d'India/fichi indiani, prickly pears

fichi in sciroppo, figs in syrup

fichi mandorlati, figs stuffed w/almonds

fico (fichi), fig

fidelanza, spaghetti in tomato
sauce in Liguria

filetti (di pomodoro), a sauce of sliced tomatoes

filetto (i), fillet or tenderloin

filu e ferru, Sardinian *grappa*

finferlo, an orange-colored mushroom

finocchiata, pork cured w/fennel & pepper

finocchio, fennel. *Finocchio selvatico* is wild fennel

finocchiona, fennel-flavored salami

fiocchetto, cold cut made from the leg of pork

fiocchi, flakes

*liver in
venice,
liver in
Milwaukee...
No grazie*

*fiasco.
the old
fashioned
straw-covered
bottle is
really
a novelty
now.*

fiocchi di granoturco, cornflakes

fiocco, ham shoulder

fior di latte, *mozzarella* made from cow's milk

fiore, flower

fiorentina, alla, w/oil, tomatoes & herbs
(sometimes w/peas or spinach)

fiori con ripieno, stuffed zucchini flowers

fiori di zucca, zucchini flowers served either filled w/cheese,
battered & fried or as a pizza topping

fiori di zucca fritti, fried zucchini flowers

flambé, flamed

focaccia, flat bread topped w/olive oil & sometimes cheese
&/or onions. Can also mean cake

focaccia barese, stuffed pizza. A specialty of Apulia

focaccia di vitello, veal patty

foglia (e), leaf

foglia di alloro/foglia di lauro, bay leaf

foglia di vite, vine leaf

foiolo, tripe (stomach lining)

folpetto, the Venetian word for baby octopus

fondo di carciofo, artichoke heart

fonduta, melted cheese (fondue)

fontina, mild cheese (soft & creamy)

forchetta, fork

formaggini d'Alpe, cow's-milk cheese found in Ticino

formaggini di capra, fresh goat's-milk cheese found in Ticino

formaggio (formaggi), cheese

formaggio di fossa, aged sheep's-milk cheese
from Le Marche

forno, al, baked

forte, strong

fracosta, rib steak

fragola (e), strawberry

fragole di bosco/fragoline di bosco, wild strawberries

fragolino, sea bream

fragolone, large strawberries

Frangelico, hazelnut-flavored cordial

frappé, milk shake

frascarelli, tiny *gnocchi*

Frascati, dry to slightly sweet white wine

frascota di bue, rib steak

frattaglie, giblets

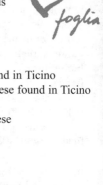

foglia

fragolone.

freddo (i)/fredda (e), cold/iced. *Tè freddo* is iced tea
fregolotta, flour, cornmeal & almond cake
fregula, dumpling soup
Freisa, dry to slightly sweet red wine
fresca (o), fresh/not cooked
freschi, wild mushrooms
fresco, al, outside (in the fresh air)
fricando, round of veal
fricassea, fricassee
fricò, cheese pancake
friggere, deep-fried (to deep fry)
frittata, omelette
frittata casalinga, plain omelette
frittata semplice, plain omelette
frittatina di patate, potato omelette
frittella (e), pancake/fritter
fritti ascolani, mixed fry of lamb chops, brains, olives
   & zucchini
fritto (a)/fritti (e), fried/deep-fried
fritto alla milanese, breaded & deep-fried
fritto alla napoletana, deep-fried fish, cheese & vegetables
fritto alla romana, deep-fried sweetbreads
fritto di verdura, fried vegetables
fritto misto, mixed deep-fried fish, meat or vegetables
fritto misto alla Fiorentina, meat & vegetable fritters
frittura, frying/fry
frittura del paese, mixed floured & fried seafood
frittura di pesce, mixed dish of fried small fish, squid &
   shrimp
frizzante, semi-sparkling wine
frolla, tender (meat)/flaky pastry
frollini, biscuits
frullato, milk shake
frullato di frutta, fruit milk shake
frumento, wheat
frumentone, corn
frutta, fruit
frutta candita, candied fruit
frutta cotta, stewed fruit
frutta fresca, fresh fruit
frutta secca, dried fruit
frutti di bosco, berries

Freschi –
FRESS - KEE

frizzante.

frutti di mare, seafood/seafood salad
fundador, w/brandy
funghetti, small mushroom-shaped pasta for soup
funghetto, al, sliced mushrooms cooked in garlic,
  onions & herbs
funghi trifolati, mushrooms sauteed in butter & garlic
fungo (funghi), mushroom
fuoco dell'Etna, strong, red Sicilian liquor
fusi, leg. *Fusi di pollo* is a chicken leg
fusilli, spiral-shaped pasta.
  Fusilli corti are short & *fusilli lunghi* are long
fusto, shank
galatina (in gelatina), pressed meat in aspic
galantina tartufata, truffles in aspic jelly
galletta, cracker/cookie. Can also refer to a mushroom or grape
galletto, chicken (cock)
Galliano, herb liqueur (yellow in color)
gallina, chicken (hen)
gallinaccio, woodcock/chanterelle mushroom
gallina faraona, guinea fowl
gallinella, waterfowl
gallinella faraona, guinea fowl
gallo, John Dory fish in Sicily
  (a firm-textured, white-fleshed
  fish w/a mild, sweet flavor
  & low fat content)
gallo cedrone, grouse (a game bird)
gamba, leg/drumstick/shank
gamba di vitello, veal shank
gamberelli, shrimp
gamberetta di rana, frogs' legs
gamberetto (i), shrimp
gambero (i), prawn/crayfish
gamberoni (gamberetti), large prawn
ganocchio, type of prawn
garetto, beef shank
garganelli, handmade pasta which is a square rolled into a tube
  (the dough is made from eggs, flour, grated *parmigiano*
  & nutmeg)
garofolato, beef stew
gaspaccio, gazpacho (the cold, tomato-based Spanish soup)
gasata/gassata, carbonated

galletto.

Gattinara, full-bodied red wine

gelatina, jelly/gelatine

gelato (i), ice cream/iced dessert

gelato al tartufo, ice cream w/chocolate sauce

gemelli, pasta made of two strands twisted around each other. The term means "twins"

genovese, alla, w/herbs (especially basil), olive oil & garlic/w/meat & onions

Genovese basil is considered the most fragrant.

germe di grano, wheat germ

germinus, almond-meringue cookies from Sardinia

germogli, sprouts

gesuita, rib steak

ghiacciato, chilled/iced

ghiaccio, ice

ghianchetti, small anchovies

ghiotta, alla, grilled or roasted

gesuito means Jesuit... presumably because the priests got the best meat.

ghiozzo, mackerel

giallo d'uova, egg yolk

gianchetti, small anchovies

gianduia, chocolate & hazelnut ice cream

gianduiotti, hazelnut-and-chocolate candies

giambonette(i)/giambonetto, boned chicken roll w/filling

giardiniera, small pieces of vegetables (a garnish)

gigantoni, large tubular pasta (means "giant")

gioddu, yogurt in Sardinia

giorno, del, of the day

gin, gin *Good Guess!*

ginepro, juniper berry

ginestrata, chicken & sweet wine soup (a sweet & sour soup). A Tuscan specialty

girarrosto, spit-roasted

girasole, sunflower

girello, rump

glassate, glazed

girasole means turns to the sun.

gnoccata al pomodoro, tomato pizza

gnocchetti, small *gnocchi*

gnocchetti alla Sarda/gnocchetti sarda, small pasta dumplings in various sauces. A specialty in Sardinia

gnocchi, flour or potato dumplings

gnocchi alla marchigiana, *gnocchi* w/chicken-giblet sauce

gnocchi alla piemontese, little balls of flour, egg & potato

gnocchi alla romana, semolina (flour) dumplings

gnocchi di patate, little balls of potato, flour & egg

gnocco fritto, deep-fried rolls of pasta

gnocco ingrassato, *focaccia* w/*prosciutto*

gnudi, means naked (w/out pasta). Stuffing only, such as in ***ravioli gnudi*** *gnudi... don't pronounce the G. NOO.DEE*

gnumariddi, a sweetbread dish

gomiti, "c"-shaped tubular pasta

gomma da masticare, chewing gum

gorgonzola, creamy, blue cheese (best-known Italian blue)

goulasch, goulash

graffo (i), doughnut *Kinda cute, hey?*

grana, mild, hard cheese (similar to *parmesan*)

granatina, steak tartare (raw ground beef). In most parts of Italy this term means Italian ice or shaved ice

granceola, spider crab. A specialty of Venice

granchio (di mare), crab

granciporro (i), crab

grande, large

granello, seed

gran farro, wheat & bean soup. Also see *farro*

grani di, seeds of...

granita, coffee or fruit syrup served over crushed ice (a "snow cone"). Originally made from snow from Mt. Etna

grano, wheat/corn

grano duro, duram wheat

grano padano, buttery, hard, seasoned cheese w/a grainy texture

grano saraceno, buckwheat

granoturco/granturco, corn on the cob

granseola, a crab found in Venice

grappa, liquor made from grape pressings. It's extremely strong *Grappa is a popular digestivo which can taste like heaven... or hell.*

grappolo, a bunch (as in a bunch of grapes)

grassi vegetali, vegetable oil

grasso (a), oily/fatty/fat/grease

graticola, grilled/broiled

gratin/gratinate, oven-browned w/cheese

gratinada, baked dish topped w/grated cheese & breadcrumbs

gratis, free

grattugiato, grated

gratuito (a), free

gremolata, minced anchovies, parsely & lemon (used as a garnish)

grenadine, veal chunks (used in casserole dishes)

gricia, alla, w/bacon, onion, cheese & chili pepper

griglia, alla, grilled (usually charcoal grilled)

grigliata mista, mixed grill of meats or fish

Grignolino, high-quality red wine

grissino (i), long, thin bread stick

grongo/gruonco/grangu, conger eel

groppo, rump (meat)

groviera/groviera svizzera, sharp
    cheese w/holes (like Swiss cheese)

guancia.

guancia, pig's cheek. *Al guanciale* means cooked w/bacon &
    onions. Also refers to the delicacy of pig's cheek

guardaroba, coat room

guarnite, alla, served w/a garnish

guazzetto, usually refers to a stew (meat or fish). In Sardinia,
    this dish almost always contains capers

gubana, sweet bread roll (dried fruit & nut strudel found in
    Friuli-Venezia Giulia)

gulyas, beef stew found in Friuli-Venezia Giulia

gusti, flavors

hasce di manzo, hamburger patty

igname, yam

impanato (a), covered in breadcrumbs

impazzata di cozze/impepata di cozze, mussels cooked in
    their own juice w/black pepper, oil, parsley & garlic

incapriata, purée of fava beans & chicory

incasciata, layered dough, meat sauce, hard-boiled eggs, cheese

incluso (a), included

Indiana, all', w/curry (Indian style)

indivia, endive/chicory

indivia Belga, Belgian endive

insaccati, salami

insalata, salad

insalata cotta...

Love it!

insalata all'americana, shrimp & mayonnaise salad

insalata caprese, tomatoes, basil & *mozzarella* salad.
    Originally a specialty on the island of Capri, but now
    found everywhere in Italy

insalata cotta, cold, cooked vegetable salad

insalata di campo, field lettuce
insalata di cesare, Caesar salad
insalata di crudita, mixed raw vegetable salad
insalata di frutti di mare, seafood salad
insalata di funghi, raw mushroom salad *not a favorite*
insalata di mare, seafood salad
insalata di patate, potato salad
insalata di petti di pollo, chicken salad w/walnuts
insalata di tonno, tuna salad
insalata di verdura cotta, boiled vegetable salad
insalata mista, mixed salad
insalata riccia, curly endive
insalata russa, diced potato & vegetable salad w/mayonnaise
insalata siciliana, salad featuring fennel & black olives
insalata verde, green salad
integrale, whole wheat
involtini al sugo, rolled veal cutlets w/ham & cheese & topped
    w/tomato sauce
involtini di cavolfiori, cabbage leaves stuffed w/meat
involtini di pesce, thin fish slices stuffed w/*prosciutto* & herbs
involtini di salvia, a deep-fried sage-leaf anchovy roll
involtini di vitello, veal roll usually stuffed w/salami & cheese
involtino (i), stuffed roll
iota, hearty vegetable soup (white beans, cabbage & bacon fat).
    A specialty of Trieste
Ischia, an island at the north end of the Gulf of Naples
I.V.A., abbreviation for Value Added Tax (V.A.T.)
jota, thick bean & sauerkraut soup (see Iota)
julienne, small strips of vegetables
kirsch, al, w/a clear cherry brandy
knoedel/knödeln, dumplings found in the
    Trentino-Alto Adige region
krapfen, doughnuts (Austrian name) *Krapfen... sounds good!*
laccetto, mackerel
lacerto, mackerel
Lacrima Christi, popular red, *Lacrima Christi –*
    white & rosé wines *tears of Christ*
Lago di Caldaro, light red wine
Lagrein Rosato, rosé wine
Lambrusco, well-known red wine (sweet)
lamelle di fegato, thin slices of liver sautéed in butter
lampasciuni, wild onions

lampone (i), raspberry

lampreda, lamprey (similar to an eel)

Lampreda. Non grazie!

lanzado, mackerel

lardarellatta alla fiamma, larded & cooked on a grill

lardo, bacon/salt pork/lard

lardone, salt pork

lardoons, cured & fried pork

lardoso, meat fat

lasagne, thin layers of dough & meat, tomatoes, cheese & sauce (baked in the oven)

lasagne al forno, large strips of pasta cooked in sauce

lasagne alla portoghese, baked custard caramel

lasagne alla vincisgrassi, baked *lasagne* w/meatballs

lasagne verdi, spinach *lasagne*

latte, milk

latte al cacao, chocolate milk

latte di mandorla, almond milk

latte intero, whole milk

latte macchiato, steamed milk w/a small amount of *espresso*. Compare this to ***espresso macchiato***

latte magro, skim milk

latterini, poached fish dish

latte scremato, skim milk

latticini, small *mozzarella* balls

lattonzolo, suckling pig

lattuga (e), lettuce

lattuga romana, romaine lettuce

lauro, bay leaf

lavarello, a type of salmon

laziale, alla, w/onions

lecca-lecca, sucker/lollypop

leccia, pompano

leggero, light or weak/light wine

legume (i), vegetable

lenticchia (e), lentil

lepre, hare

lepre in salmì, marinated hare ("jugged hare")

leprotto, young hare

lessato (a), boiled

lesso, boiled. This can also refer to meat or fish stew

letterato, small tuna fish

lievito, yeast/baking powder

Latte. generally not drunk by the glass.

limonata.

lievito di birra, brewer's yeast

limonata, lemonade/lemon soda

limoncello, alcohol & lemon-zest drink. This is
   called *limoncino* in the Cinque Terre

limone (i), lemon. *Al limone* means w/lemon juice

lingua, tongue

linguine, flat noodles

liquore (i), liqueur. *Liquore Strega* is a sweet herb liqueur

liquoroso, fortified dessert wine

liscia/lisce, refers to smooth pasta (w/out ridges)

liscio, straight. *Brodo liscio* is plain broth

lissa, pompano in Venice

lista, menu. *Lista dei vini* is the wine list

livornese, alla, usually beans in tomato sauce w/celery
   & onions

locale, local

lodigiano, a type of *parmesan* cheese

Lombarda, alla, served fried in butter w/lemon juice & parsley

lombata, loin/leg. *Lombata di maiale* is a pork chop. *Lombata
   di vitello* is a grilled veal chop

lombata ai sassi, floured steak sautéed in butter w/sage & fried
   potatoes

lombatine, tenderloin or cut of meat for filet mignon

lombello, loin/leg

lombo di manzo, beef loin/sirloin

lombo di vitello, veal sirloin

lonza, loin

lucanica, spicy sausage

lucerna (e), grouper

luccio, pike

lucullo, alla, raw beef (steak tartare)

Lugana, dry white wine

Lumaca.

luganega, pork sausage. This spicy sausage from Basilicata
   has many similar spellings such as *luganica* & *lucanica*

lumaca (lumache), snail. *Lumache* also refers to snail-shaped
   pasta. *Lumachine* is a small version of this pasta
   used in soup

lumache alla Bourguignonne, snails w/garlic butter
   ("Burgundy snails")

lunga, long (as in long pasta or *pasta lunga*)

lungo, lighter *espresso*

lupo di mare, sea perch

luvasu, sea bream

maccarello, mackerel

maccarones con bottarga, Sardinian pasta w/fish eggs

maccaruni di casa, Sicilian pasta dish served
w/tomato & meat sauce

maccheroni, *macaroni*

maccheroni al pettine, pasta w/ridges usually served w/ragù

macchiato, *espresso* w/a small drop of milk

macco di fave, broad bean, onion & tomato soup

macedonia di frutta, fruit salad

macedonia di legumi, mixed cooked vegetables

macinata, ground. *La carne macinata* is ground beef

madera, al, cooked in Madeira wine

mafaldine, pasta ribbons

maggiorana, marjoram

magro, dish w/no meat/lean.
Ravioli di magro is stuffed pasta
w/herbs & *ricotta* cheese

marjoram is a member of the oregano family.

maiale, pork

maionese, mayonnaise

mais, corn

malfatti di ricotta, *ricotta gnocchi. Malfatti* means badly
made, a reference to the handmade dumplings in this dish

malloreddus, flavored dumplings found in Sardinia

malloreddus all'oristanese, saffron-flavored dumplings w/a
sauce of Swiss chard, cream & eggs

maltagliata, *macaroni*

mammole, artichokes   *mammole.*

mancia, tip

mandarino (i), tangerine/mandarin

mandorla (e)/mandorlata, almond

manicotti, stuffed (w/cheese & meats), baked pasta dish

mantecato, whipped ice cream. This also refers to a way to
prepare cod

manzo (di bue), beef

manzo arrosto ripieno, stuffed roast

manzo lesso, boiled beef

manzo salato, corned beef

manzo stufato al vino rosso, beef stewed in red wine

maraschino/marasco, w/Maraschino (cherry-flavored liqueur)

marchigiana, alla, a dish in the style of Le Marche (one of the
regions of Italy), usually cooked w/chicken giblet sauce

mare, di, of the sea

mare-monti, a dish served w/mushrooms & shrimp

margarina, margarine

margherita, this term is used to describe a pizza w/tomato, *mozzarella* & basil

marinara, alla, usually, but not always, means in tomato sauce (usually w/garlic & onions). The term means "of the sea" or "sailor's style," so can also refer to a dish w/seafood

marinata (o), marinated

maritozzo, soft bread roll

marmellata, marmalade/jam

marmellata d'arance, marmalade

marrone (i), chestnut. *Marrons glaces* are candied chestnuts

Marsala, fortified dessert wine from Sicily

marsala, al, in a Marsala (fortified dessert wine) sauce

Martini, vermouth

mascarpone, a soft, very creamy, fresh cheese (even for cheese, it's high fat)

masenette, tiny crabs eaten whole (w/the shell)/Venetian word for small soft-shelled crabs

matriciana, bacon, tomato & spices sauce

mattone, al, pounded flat (usually chicken) & roasted in a brick oven

mazza da tamburo, a parasol-shaped mushroom

mazzancelle/mazzancolle, very large prawns

mazzancougni, very large prawns

medaglione, medallions

medallione, a grilled ham & cheese sandwich

media, medium

mela (e), apple

melacotogna, quince

melagrana, pomegranate

melanzana (e), eggplant

eggplant is a member of the same family as tomatoes, potatoes & peppers.

melanzane al funghetto, sautéed eggplant

melanzane alla Napoletana, eggplant Neopolitan style (layered w/cheese & tomato puree & baked in an oven)

melanzane alla parmigiana, eggplant *parmesan* (w/tomatoes & *parmesan* cheese)

melanzane ripiene, stuffed eggplant

melassa, molasses

meliga, cornmeal

melone, melon/canteloupe

menta, mint
mentine, mints
menù, menu
menù a prezzo fisso, set menu
menù turistico, fixed-price menu
merca, roast fish dish from Sardinia
merenda, late morning/afternoon snack
meringa, meringue
meringa chantilly, meringue shells filled w/whipped cream
meringato/meringhe/meringua, meringue
merlango, hake/cod/whiting
merlano, whiting, cod or hake
merluzzo, cod
messicani, veal scallops dish/veal rolls
mesticanza, mixture of salad greens
metà, half
mezzo (a), half
mezzelune ai pinoli, pine-nut cookies from Umbria
mezze maniche, short tubular pasta
miascia, bread & fruit pudding
midollo, marrow
miele, honey
miglio, millet

millefoglie means a thousand leaves

milanese, alla, battered w/eggs & breadcrumbs & fried
Millefiori, herb-based liqueur
millefoglie, puff pastry/napoleon
millerighe, ridged tubular pasta (means "thousand lines"
   after the ridges in the pasta)
mimosa, spongecake & whipped-cream dessert
minerale, mineral (as in *acqua minerale* or mineral water)
minestra (minestre), soup (usually thick soup)
minestra al farro, soup made with *farro* (a wheat similar to
   spelt)
minestra di cipolle, onion soup
minestra di fagioli, bean soup
minestra di farina tostata, toasted-flour soup
minestra di farro, soup made with *farro* (a wheat)
minestra di funghi, cream of mushroom soup
minestra di lenticchie, lentil soup
minestra di pomodoro, tomato soup
minestra di riso, rice soup
minestra in brodo, broth w/noodles or rice & chicken livers

minestra maritata, meat broth & vegetable soup
minestre di piscialetto, dandelion-greens soup
minestrina, soup (usually clear)
minestrone, bean & vegetable soup w/noodles, vegetables, rice
minestrone alla genovese, vegetable soup
    w/*macaroni* & spinach
minestrone verde, thick vegetable soup w/herbs & beans
mirabella (e), small plum
mirtillo (i), blueberry. The word *mirtilli* is also used for berries
    in general & for cranberries
mischianza, salad of wild greens, herbs & edible flowers
misoltini, salted & dried shad (fish)
misticanza, salad of wild greens, herbs & edible flowers
misto/misti, mixed
misto del golfo/misto del paese, mixed floured & fried seafood
misto mare, mixed floured & fried seafood
mitilo, mussel
moka, mocha
molto, very
montanara, alla, has many meanings but generally means
    w/red wine sauce or w/vegetables
montare, to whip (usually refers to cream)
montebianco/Mont Blanc, pyramid of sweetened chestnuts &
    whipped cream (named after Mont Blanc) *Mont Blanc*
Montepulciano, full-bodied, dry red wine *is the*
montone, mutton *French side of*
monzittas, snails in Sardinia *Monte Bianco*
mora (e), blackberry *mountain.*
mormora, small fish found in the Mediterranean
mortadella, luncheon meat w/pistachio nuts & peppercorns
morto, pot roast
mosca, con la, a drink (usually *Sambuca*) served "w/the
    fly"(*con la mosca*). The "fly" is a coffee bean in the glass
moscardino (i), small squid
Moscatello/Moscato, muscatel (table & dessert white & red
    wines from the muscat grape)
mostarda, mustard. This word is rarely used. Most use *senape*
mostarda di frutta, candied fruits in syrup/preserved fruits in
    a mustard sauce/fruit chutney
mousse al cioccolato, chocolate mousse
mozzarella, a soft, fresh (unripened), slightly sweet cheese
mozzarella di bufala, *mozzarella* made from buffalo milk

mozzarella in carrozza, fried *mozzarella* sandwich
(means "in a carriage")

muddica, breadcrumbs in Sicily

muggine, grey mullet

muscoletti, shank

muscoli, mussels. This word is rarely used. Most use *cozze*

muscoli alla marinara, steamed mussels dish

musetto, salami

napoletana, ("Naples-style") w/tomato sauce (w/out meat)

nasello, whiting/hake/cod

naturale, plain/natural

nave, di, w/seafood

navone (i), turnip

`nduja, Calabrian pork sausage

Nebbiolo, full-bodied dry red wine

nepitella, an herb similar to mint

nero (a), black

nervetti, calf's foot dish (tendons of calves' feet).
A Venetian specialty

Navone.

nervetti...
I don't
think so.

nespola, medlar (a tart fruit)

nidi di rondine, pasta rolls

nocciola (e), hazelnut

noccioline americane, peanuts

nocciole, nuts

noce (i), nut/walnut. Can also refer to the top round of veal

noce di cocco, coconut

nocelli, walnut-raisin cookies

noce moscata, nutmeg

nocepesca, nectarine

noci d'anacardo, cashews

Nocillo/Nocino, liquor made from walnuts

nodino (i), chop/small grilled pork chop

non, not

non fumatori, no smoking

non gassata, still or not carbonated

nonna, alla, this can be any sauce served w/pasta. The term
means "grandmother" & there are as many variations of
"alla nonna" as there are grandmothers

norcina, sausage & cheese sauce. After the town of Norcia

Norma, alla, this usually refers to a dish served w/eggplants,
tomatoes, basil & sometimes *ricotta* cheese

nostrale/nostrano, home-grown/local

novellame, a spread of salted anchovies & *peperoncino* sauce
novello/novelli, fresh/tender
o, or
oca, goose
occhiate, orata (a fish)
occhi di lupo, small tubular pasta
   "wolves' eyes")
olio, oil/olive oil
olio d'arachide, peanut oil
olio da tavola, salad oil
olio di cartamo, safflower oil
olio di girasole, sunflower oil
olio di grano/olio di granturco, corn oil
olio di palma, palm oil
olio di semi, seed oil/corn oil
olio d'oliva, olive oil
olio santo, chili-infused oil
oliva (e), olive (*nere*, black, *verdi,* green)
olive agrodolci, olives in sugar & vinegar
olive ascolane, large green olives. *Olive all'ascolana*,
   in Le Marche, olives stuffed w/meat & fried in olive oil
ombra, glass of wine in Venice. This word is usually used at a
   bar & not at a restaurant
ombrina, umbrine (seafood/bass)
omelette, omelette
omelette casalinga, plain omelette
omelette semplice, plain omelette
oranciata, orangeade
orata, a fish found in the Mediterranean (bream/gilthead)
oratino, a small *orata* fish
orecchiette, small ear-shaped pasta
orecchiette con le cime di rapa, small ear-shaped pasta
   w/turnips. A specialty in Apulia
origano, oregano
ortaggi, vegetables/greens/herbs
Orvieto, light, dry, white wine from Orvieto in Umbria
orzata, almond or barley-flavored water
orzetto, barley & potato soup
orzo (i), rice-shaped pasta. Can also refer to barley
osso, bone
ossobuco (ossibuchi), braised veal-shank dish. You may be
   given a marrow spoon to eat the marrow in the bone

*Olio d'oliva
we never leave
Italy without
a bottle.*

ossobuco alla milanese, veal shank, tomatoes, garlic & wine

ostrica (ostriche), oyster

ovalina, a type of *mozzarella* cheese

ovolo (i), a rare (& delicious) mushroom w/an orange & scarlet color. Sometimes called Caesar's mushroom

pacchetto, package

paciugo, parfait

padella, in, fried

paesana, alla, usually means served w/bacon (or sausage), potatoes, carrots & other vegetables

paeta, spit-roasted turkey

pagaro/pagello, sea bream/porgy

paglia e fieno, pasta dish w/yellow (egg) & green (spinach) pasta (means "straw & hay")

pagliarino, soft, mild cheese

pagliata, a dish containing organ meat

pagnotta, loaf

pagnotta del cacciatore, game birds roasted in dough

pagro, sea bream/porgy

paiata, spit-roasted turkey

paillard, beef rib steak or veal cutlet pounded thin & grilled

pajata, a dish containing organ meat

palamito, bonito fish

palemone, prawns

pallina, scoop (as in scoop of ice cream). The word really means "marble"

palomba/palombaccia, pigeon

palombacci, an Umbrian dish of small birds cooked whole on a spit

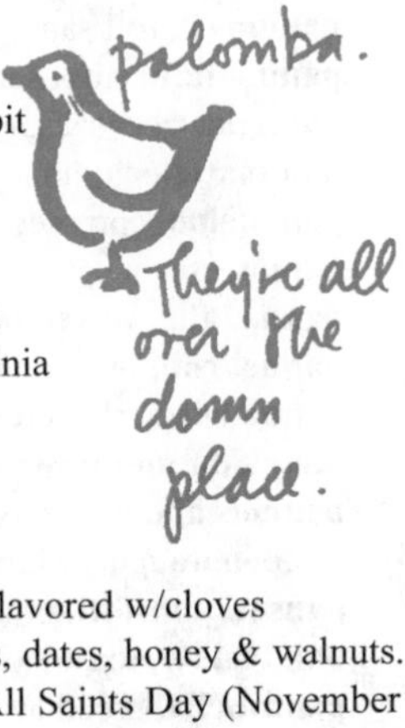

palombo, dogfish/shark found in Sicily

panafittas, dried bread broken into pieces & boiled (like pasta), then served in a tomato sauce in Sardinia

panardo, a thirty-course feast served in Abruzzo

panata, bread soup

pancetta, bacon (cured pork belly)

pancetta arrotolata, rolled bacon flavored w/cloves

pan có Santi, sweet bread w/raisins, dates, honey & walnuts. "Saints' bread" is eaten around All Saints Day (November 1)

pan di Genova, almond cake

[handwritten margin note: palomba. They're all over the damn place.]

pan di Spagna, spongecake

pandolce, cake w/dried fruit

pandoro (di Verona), star-shaped light cake w/sugar topping

pane, bread/loaf

pane bianco, white bread

pane bigio, whole-wheat bread

pane carasau, flat crispy bread found in Sardinia. Also known as *carta da musica* (music paper)

pane di segale, rye bread

pane e coperto, the charge for bread & for sitting at the table

pane frattau, *pane carasau* topped w/tomato sauce, grated cheese & a fried egg. A specialty in Sardinia

pane grattugiato, breadcrumbs

pane integrale, whole-wheat bread

panelle, chickpea fritters

pane nero, dark bread

pane pepato, gingerbread

pane piccante, gingerbread

pane scuro, pumpernickel bread

pane toscano, sourdough bread

pane tostato, toast

panettone, spiced cakes or coffeecakes w/candied fruits

panforte, flat, hard fruitcake

pan grattato, breadcrumbs

panicielli d'uva passula, grapes wrapped in leaves & baked

panino (i), roll/sandwich

panino imbottito, sandwich

paniscia, rice, sausage & bean soup

pan matteloch, honey bread found in the lake country

pan meino, cornmeal bread/cake (millet bread) w/elderflowers

panna, cream

panna, alla, served in a cream sauce or w/creamy gravy

panna, con, in a cream sauce/w/cream

panna cotta, rich cream custard

panna da montare/panna montata, whipped cream

pannocchia, corn on the cob

panpepato, gingerbread or hazelnut cake

pansoti/pansotti, triangular-shaped filled pasta

pan tostato, toast

panzanella, bread & vegetable salad

panzerotti, baked (or deep-fried) dough filled w/pork, cheese, tomatoes or other ingredients

*Pane.
the Italians,
like the French
are fiercely
proud of their
bread.*

panzoni, stuffed ravioli dish

paparot, cornmeal & spinach dish from Friuli-Venezia Giulia

pappa al pomodoro, tomato & bread soup

pappardelle, long, flat, wide pasta

pappardelle al sugo di lepre/pappardelle alla lepre, strips of pasta w/rabbit sauce

paprica, paprika

pardulas, Sardinian pastries filled w/cream cheese

parigina, hamburger buns. In Sicily, this refers to bread

parmigiana, alla, w/*parmesan* cheese & tomatoes

parmigiana di melanzane, baked slices of eggplant layered w/*parmesan* cheese, tomatoes & *mozzarella*

parmigiano, *parmesan* cheese usually served grated

parmigiano-reggiano, the "real" name for *parmesan* cheese

partenopea, means "Naples' style," the same as *Napolitana*

Pasqualina, "Easter style" which can mean roasted in an oven w/olive oil, onion, garlic, black olives & celery. **Torta Pasqualina** is a pie featuring artichokes

passate di legumi, puree of vegetables

passatelli, pasta of *parmesan* cheese, eggs & breadcrumbs

passato, puree

passato di verdura, cream of vegetable soup

passera di mare, flounder

passera pianuzza, flounder

passerino, flounder

pasta, pasta (dough made of flour, oil, butter, eggs & water). The first course in Italy. If you find -*ette* or -*ini* after pasta, this means a smaller version of pasta. For example, *pennette* & *pennini* are smaller versions of *penne*. If you find -*oni* after pasta, this means a large pasta like *rigatoni*. *Pasta* that starts w/*taglia* is made of long, thin strips. *Pasta* can also mean pastry

pasta al forno, any pasta mixed w/a sauce & baked

pasta alla Norma, pasta w/tomatoes, basil & eggplant topped w/*ricotta* cheese

pasta asciutta, any pasta not eaten in soup

pasta con le sarde, pasta w/fresh sardines

pasta d'arachide, peanut butter

pasta di olive, olive paste

pasta e ceci, pasta & chickpea soup

pasta e fagioli, pasta & bean soup

pasta frolla, puff pastry
pasta in brodo, pasta in broth
pasta 'ncasciata, pasta baked w/eggplant, salami, tomato/basil
pasta reale (paste reali), marzipan cake
   (means "royal pastry")
pasta sfoglia, puff-pastry dough
paste, pastries
pastella, batter for frying
pasticceria (e), pastry
pasticcetti, small tarts
pasticciata, baked pasta (in a casserole)
pasticcini da te, teacakes/small pastries
pasticcino (i), cake/small pastry/tart
pasticcio, pastry/pie. Also the Venetian word for baked lasagne
pasticcio di maccheroni, sweet pie containing meat sauce
pastiera napoletana, *ricotta* cheese-filled pastry
pastina, small pasta usually used in soup
pastina in brodo, pasta served in soup
pastissa, pot pie
pasto, meal
patata (e), potato
patate al lesso, boiled potatoes
patate al ghiotto/patate alla ghiottona, stuffed baked potatoes
patate americane, sweet potato
patate arroste, roasted potatoes
patate bollite, boiled potatoes
patate dolci, sweet potato
patate fritte, fried potatoes/french fries
patate in padella, potatoes fried in a pan
patate lesse, boiled potatoes
patate novelle, new potatoes
patate rosolate, roasted potatoes
patate saltate, potatoes sliced & sautéed
patate tenere, new potatoes
patatine fritte, french fries/chips
patatine novelle, small roasted potatoes
pate/paterini, pâté
pecora, sheep/ewe
pecorino, hard, sharp cheese usually served grated.
   Pecorino alla griglia is a Sardinian specialty of grilled
   pecorino cheese
pellegrine, scallops

Anti-before
pasto-meal
antipasto.

penne, tube-shaped pasta (cut at an angle)
pennette, smaller version of *penne*
penneziti, larger version of *penne*
pennoni, the largest version of *penne*
peoci, mussels. Also the Venetian word for "head lice"
pepata di cozze, mussels in a black pepper, oil & garlic sauce
pepato, peppered
pepe, black pepper
pepe di Giamaica, allspice
peperonata, tomatoes, peppers & onion stewed together
peperoncino (i), small, spicy pickled pepper
peperone (i), pepper
peperoni alla brace, roasted marinated peppers
peperoni imbottiti, stuffed peppers
peperoni ripieni, stuffed peppers
peperoni rossi, red peppers
peperoni sott'aceto, pickled chilis
peperoni verdi, green peppers
pera (e), pear
perciatelli, hollow spaghetti noodles
per contorno, meal includes salad or side dish
pere helene/pere elena, poached pear served in vanilla ice
     cream & topped w/chocolate sauce
pernice, partridge
persico, perch
pesca (pesche), peach
pesca melba, peaches in syrup w/ice cream & whipped cream
pescatora/pescatore, seafood sauce for pasta & rice dishes
pescatrice, angler fish
pesce, fish
pesce carpionata, marinated fish in herbs
pesce in saor, fish in a sauce of onion, raisin, pine nut &
     vinegar. A specialty in Veneto
pesce persico, perch
pesce San Pietro, John Dory fish (a firm-textured, white-
     fleshed fish w/a mild, sweet flavor and low fat content)
pesce sciabola, an eel-like fish
pesce serra, bluefish
pesce spada, swordfish
pesce stocco, cod
pesce turchino, mackerel
pesche, peaches

pesche aurora, spongecake soaked in peach liqueur

pesto, basil, oil, garlic & pine-nut sauce

petonchio, scallops

petroniana, alla, can mean many things, most frequently breaded & fried & topped w/melted cheese

pettine (i), small scallop

petto, breast (of poultry)

petto alla principessa, chicken floured & fried in butter & served w/an egg on top

petto all'arancio, chicken in an orange sauce

petto di pollo, chicken breast

peverada, chicken liver & anchovy sauce *only for the brave.*

pezzenta, pork salami

pezzo, piece

piacere, of your own choice (your pleasure)

piadina, soft, flat bread

pianuzza, flounder/halibut

piastra, grilled on a flat steel plate

piattino, saucer

piatto (i), dish/plate. *Piatti freddi* means cold dishes

piatto del giorno, dish of the day

piccante, highly seasoned (hot)

piccata (e), veal scallop

piccata all'allegro, veal scallop fried in butter w/lemon juice

piccata alla Lombarda, veal scallop fried in butter w/lemon juice & parsley

piccata di vitello, veal cooked in lemon & parsley

piccatina, veal scallop dish

piccioncino, young pigeon

piccione, pigeon

piccione selvatico, wild pigeon

piccolo (i)/piccola (e), small

pici, eggless pasta

piede (i), foot

piemontese, sauce w/truffles ("Piedmont style")

pietanza, dish/main course

pignata, lamb or goat w/herbs. A specialty from Basilicata named after the terra-cotta pot it's cooked in

pimento, pimento/allspice

pimiento, sweet red peppers

pinoccate/pinocchiata, almond & pine-nut cake

pinolata, pine-nut dessert cake found in Tuscany

pinolo (i), pine nut
Pinot Grigio, light, fruity white wine
pinsimonio/pinzimonio, oil, pepper & salt dressing/oil &
   mustard dressing for dipping
pinza, yellow flour, pine nut & raisin cake from Veneto
pipe, pasta similar to *lumache* (a snail-shaped pasta)
pisello (i), pea
pistacchi, pistachio nuts
pitta, pizza either stuffed or
   topped with many ingredients.
   Popular in Calabria
piviere, plover (bird)
pizza, pizza
pizza alla marinara, the "true"
   pizza: tomato, olive oil & oregano
pizza alla napoletana, pizza w/cheese, capers, tomatoes,
   anchovies, olives & *mozzarella*
pizza alla siciliana, pizza w/salami or ham, anchovies, olives,
   tomatoes & *mozzarella*
pizza bianca, pizza bread topped w/sea salt & olive oil
pizza capricciosa, same as *pizza quattro stagioni*
pizza di Pasqua, cheese bread
pizzaiola, w/tomato & garlic sauce
pizzaiolo, pizza man (the maker of pizzas)
pizza margherita, pizza w/tomato, basil & *mozzarella*
pizza marinara, pizza w/garlic, oil & oregano. Can also refer
   to a pizza w/black olives, anchovies, tomatoes & capers
pizza quattro stagioni, w/seafood, cheese,
   artichokes & ham in four sections.
   Means "four seasons" & is a pizza which has a
   different topping for each quarter
pizza rustica, common in central Italy; serves large rectangular
   pizzas with thicker crusts and more toppings than usually
   found in a *pizzeria*. You can order as much as you want, and
   pay by weight
pizzelle, small (fried) pizzas
pizzetta, small pizza
pizzoccheri, pasta made w/buckwheat flour
polenta, cornmeal mush
polenta concia, *polenta* w/cheese
polenta di grano saraceno, buckwheat *polenta*
polenta dolce, sweet *polenta* dessert

Pizza... Man's highest culinary achievement. (handwritten note)

77

polenta e osei, *polenta* w/roast fowl

polenta grassa, butter, fontina cheese & *polenta*

polenta pasticciata, *polenta* served w/meat sauce, cheese, mushrooms & sauce (*polenta* pie)

polipetto (i), small squid/baby octopus

polipo (i)/polpo (i), octopus

pollame, poultry

pollastra/pollastrello, young chicken

pollo al mattone/pollastrino al mattone,
chicken pounded flat & roasted in a brick oven

polletto, spring chicken

pollo, chicken

pollo alla diavola, highly spiced, grilled chicken

pollo alla Marengo, sautéed chicken dish with many ingredients (usually tomatoes, mushrooms & onions). The dish takes its name from the town of Marengo, where Napoleon defeated the Austrians

pollo alla romana, fried chicken pieces, bacon & garlic

pollo all'arrabbiata, "Enraged chicken" (a spicy chicken dish)

pollo arrosto, roasted chicken

pollo fritto Fiorentina, chicken marinated in oil, lemon juice & herbs

pollo in bellavista, roasted chicken dish w/vegetables

pollo novello, spring chicken

pollo piccata al Marsala, chicken pounded thin & fried in butter & Marsala wine

pollo scarpariello, boneless chicken w/lemon, garlic & parsley

polpa, lean meat/flesh

polpetielle, baby octopus

polpetta (e) di carne, meatball

polpetti affogati, small octopuses cooked w/tomatoes (means "drowned octopuses")

polpettine (i), meatball. *Polpettine di pesce* is a seafood ball

polpettone, meat loaf

polpi arricciati, "curled octopus." An octopus dish in which the octopus is curled by beating & twirling it in a basket

polpo, octopus

polpo in purgatorio, octopus sautéed in oil w/tomatoes & peppers

pomi d'oro, the original name for tomato (means "golden apple"). It's believed that the tomato arrived in Europe w/a golden color that turned red under the hot Mediterranean sun

(handwritten margin note) pollo al mattone is a favorite!

pommarola (salsa di), tomato sauce

pomo (i), apple

pomodoro (i), tomato

pomodoro, al, w/tomato sauce

pomodoro doppio (concentrato), thick tomato paste

pomodoro pelati, peeled tomatoes in their own juice

pomodoro pumate, sun-dried tomato

pomodoro super cirio, thick tomato pureé

pomodori con tonno, tomatoes stuffed w/tuna

pomodori secchi, sun-dried tomatoes

pompelmo, grapefruit

popone, melon

porcecellino, suckling pig

porceddu/porcheddu, Sardinian word for roast suckling pig

porcello, young pig

porchetta, roast suckling pig stuffed w/herbs

porcini, mushrooms (the wild mushroom boletus)

porco, pork

porri dorati, battered & deep-fried leeks

porro (i), leek

portacenere, ashtray

portafoglio, veal cutlet stuffed
w/herbs, cheese & other ingredients.
This is also the word for wallet

[handwritten note:] porta cenere Can't get away from it in Italy.

portata (e), course

porto, port

portoghese, usually means
w/tomato sauce

porzione, portion

posillipo, seafood sauce

praio, dorade (fish)/gilt-head bream

pranzo, lunch/dinner

presnitz, dessert made w/dried fruit from
Fruili-Venezia Giulia

prezzemolo (i), parsley

prezzo, price

prezzo fisso, fixed price

prima colazione, breakfast

primavera, spring vegetables & cream sauce

primizie, spring vegetables or fruit

primo, first (as in *primo piatto*, first course)

principale, main (as in *piatto principale*, main course)

profiterole, filled ice-cream puff topped w/chocolate sauce & whipped cream

prosciutto, aged & cured ham

prosciutto affumicato, cured, smoked ham

prosciutto cotto, cooked or boiled ham

prosciutto crudo, salted, cured ham/Parma ham

prosciutto di cinghiale, smoked wild boar

prosciutto di San Daniele, a cured ham named after a town in the Friuli-Venezia Giulia region

prosciutto e melone, ham & melon

prosciutto di Parma, Parma ham (famous cured ham of Parma)

Prosecco, sparkling white wine from Veneto

provatura, soft, mild & sweet cheese

provenzale, onions, black olives, tomato & mushroom sauce

provolone, mild buffalo cheese

provolone dolce, mild, white, medium-hard cheese

provolone piccante, sharp cheese

prugna (e), plum

prugna secca (prugne secche), prune

pumaruolo/pumaruoro, tomato in Sicily & Campania

pumate, sun-dried tomatoes

punta di vitello, veal brisket

puntarelle, a salad green

punte di asparagi, asparagus tips

Punt e Mes, orange-flavored vermouth (drunk before meals)

puntino, a, medium done

punto, breast. *Punto* also means medium rare

purea, pureed/mashed

purea di fave, a puree of broad beans often spread on bread

purè di patate, mashed potatoes

puttanaio, a stew-like ratatouille (means "prostitute stew")

puttanesca, tomato, black olives, anchovies, capers & garlic sauce (the term means "prostitute"). Allegedly named because prostitutes could prepare this quick meal between "customers"

quadrello, pork loin

quadrello d'agnello, rack of lamb

quadretti, refers to small squares of pasta

Absolute favorite

quadrucci, square-shaped pasta for soup

quaglia (e), quail

quattro formaggi, four cheeses

quattro spezie, four spices combined
(pepper, cloves, juniper & nutmeg)

quattro stagioni, pizza
w/seafood, cheese,
artichokes & ham
in four sections

*Quattro Stagione
means
Four Seasons*

rabarbaro, rhubarb. This can also refer to an
after-dinner liqueur

radiatori, pasta shaped like a radiator

radicchio, red endive/red chicory (bitter red lettuce)

rafano, horseradish

ragnetto, rolls

ragno, sea bass

ragno di mare, spider crab

ragù, tomato-based meat sauce

ragusano, hard, slightly sweet cheese

ramolaccio, horseradish

ranapescatrice, angler fish

rane, frogs or frogs' legs

rannocchi, frog or frogs' legs

rapa (e), turnip

rape rosse, beet root

raspante, farm-raised (usually chicken). Means "scratching"

Ratafia, black-cherry liqueur

rattatuia, ratatouille

ravanada, horseradish sauce

ravanello (i), radish

raviggiolo, goat's-milk cheese

ravioli, squares of pasta w/stuffing. *Raviolini* are half-circle
stuffed pasta

ravioli gnudi, ravioli stuffing (without the pasta)

ravioli verdi, spinach ravioli

razza, ray

recchie/recchietelle, the word in Apulia for *orecchiette* (ear-
shaped pasta)

remolazzitt, radish

rene (i), kidney

ribes, currants

ribes neri, black currants

Rana.

ribes rossi, red currants

ribollita, vegetable soup (which means "reboiled") thickened
w/bread. There are many versions of this Tuscan soup

ricciarelli, marzipan &/or almond biscuits

riccio (di mare)/ricci (di mare), sea urchin

ricciola, amberjack (fish)

riccioli, small, curly pasta

riccolo, curly endive

ricotta, similar to cottage cheese, sweetened when
used in desserts

ricotta al maraschino, *ricotta* cheese w/maraschino

rigaglia (e), giblets

rigata (e), refers to ridges in pasta

rigatoni, large tube-shaped pasta (always has ridges)

rigatoni alla Norma, a Sicilian dish of pasta w/eggplant &
tomato sauce

righini, bluegill

ripieno/ripiene, stuffed

riserva, mature wine

risi e bisi, creamy rice w/green peas.
Bisi is the Venetian word for peas

riso (i), rice

riso ai gamberi, rice w/shrimp

riso alla genovese, rice w/sauce of minced beef (or veal)
w/vegetables

riso alla Greca, rice, vegetables & sausage dish (Greek style)

riso alla milanese, golden rice dish from Milan
featuring saffron

riso alla pilota, rice w/a sausage meat sauce

riso e ceci, broth of rice & chickpeas w/tomatoes & spices

riso in bianco, white rice w/butter

riso in cagnone, boiled rice topped w/*parmesan* cheese

riso mantecado, rice cooked in butter & milk

riso nero, black rice. The rice is made black from squid ink

risoni, rice-shaped pasta for soup

risotto, creamy rice dish w/various ingredients. Served as a
first course, *i primi*, after the *antipasto*

risotto ai fiori di zucca, rice dish made w/a heavy cream base
& zucchini flowers stirred in w/*parmesan*. A Ticino specialty

risotto alla certosina, creamy rice dish w/shrimp, mushrooms,
peas & sometimes frogs' legs

risotto alla mantovana, rice dish w/salami & *parmesan* cheese

Ribollita
means
Reboiled.

Risie Bisi...
another
favorite.

risotto alla milanese, rice w/butter, saffron, beef,
zucchini & *parmesan*

risotto alla pescatora, spicy rice w/seafood

risotto alla romana, rice usually w/lamb & potatoes

risotto alla valdostana, rice w/cheese & wine

risotto alla Valenciana, the same dish as Spanish *paella*

risotto alla Veneta, rice w/mussels

risotto alla veronese, rice & ham w/mushrooms

risotto al salto, crisp rice cake

risotto di frutti di mare, rice w/shellfish

risotto di peoci, rice w/mussels

risotto nero, black *risotto*.
Squid or cuttlefish ink makes the rice black

ristretto, reduced broth

robiola, soft, mild & slightly sweet cheese

robiolina, sheep's-milk cheese

rocciate, pastry w/fruit & nuts

rognoncini, kidneys

rognoncini al vino bianco, kidneys in white-wine sauce

rognone (i), kidney

rolatine di vitello, veal cutlets stuffed w/ham &/or cheese

rollè, roll

romagnola, typically, a sauce of tomato, garlic & parsley

romana, alla, a catch-all term that literally means
"Roman style"

rombo, turbot

rosato, rosé

rosbif, roast beef

roscioli, red mullet in Abruzzo

rosé, rosé (blush) wine

rosmarino, rosemary

Rosolio, sweet liqueur

rospo, monkfish/angler fish. *Rospo* also means toad,
so this fish is often referred to as *pesce rospo*

rosso, red

Rosso Antico, cherry-flavored vermouth

rotella, round

rotelle/rotelline, wheel-shaped pasta

rotini, spiral-shaped pasta

rotolo, rolled meat w/stuffing.
Rotolo di spinaci is a spinach roll (pasta w/spinach)

rovi, blackberries

rucola, arugula, also called rocket salad

rughetta, salad green

rujolos, Sardinian sweet-cheese fritters

rum, rum

ruote di carro, pasta in the shape of a wheel (same as *rotelle*)

rustica, alla, usually means a pepper & olive sauce, but can mean many things

sagro, sea bream

salame (i), smoked sausage. *Salamino* is a small salami

salame di cioccolato/ salame al cioccolato, chocolate cake in the shape of (& looks like) a salami

Salame!

salamino piccante, pepperoni

salatina, greens for salad

salatini, crackers/snacks

salato, salted/salami

salciccia, sausage

sale, salt

salmi, in, marinated in wine, garlic & herbs (usually w/game)

salmone, salmon. *Salmoncino* is young salmon

salsa, sauce. *Salsa balsamella* is béchamel (white) sauce

salsa bianca, white sauce

salsa di pommarola, tomato sauce

salsa di salsiccie, sausage sauce

salsa per la cacciagione, "hunters' sauce" for cooking game

salsa tartara, tartar sauce

salsa verde, parsley-based green sauce (w/oil, lemon juice, capers & garlic)

salsicce di maiale, pork sausages

salsiccia (e), fresh sausage

saltato (i)/saltata (e), sautéed

saltimbocca, veal cutlet wrapped around ham & sage

Saltimbocca means jump in the mouth.

salumi, sausages

salumi cotti, cooked sausages & cured meats

salvia, sage

salvietta, napkin (paper)

Sambuca, anise-flavored liqueur. When served *con la mosca* ("w/the fly"), the "fly" is a coffee bean in the glass

sanato, young calf

sandwich, sandwich

sangiovese, primary grape of Chianti wine

sangue, al, rare

Sanguinaccio, blood sausage (black pudding).
  Also a chocolate spread made from chocolate & pigs' blood

San Pietro, John Dory fish (a firm-textured, white-fleshed fish
  w/a mild, sweet flavor and low fat content)

San Severo, dry red wine from southern Italy

saor, sweet & sour sauce

sapa, thick sauce made from the juice of freshly pressed grapes

saporito (a), mild/tasty

sarago (saraghi), bluegill

sarda (e)/sardine, sardine

sarda, alla, tomato & meat sauce w/herbs & red wine
  ("Sardinian style")

sarde a beccaficu, sardines usually stuffed w/pine nuts &
  raisins. A Sicilian specialty

sardella, fried baby fish minced w/olive oil & powdered
  peppers from Calabria

sardina, small sardine

sardo, hard, aromatic cheese

sardoncini, little sardines

sartù, baked rice dish w/tomatoes, meatballs & mushrooms

savarin, cake baked in a ring mold & soaked in liquor. The
  center is filled w/fruit & whipped cream

sbrisolona, flour, cornmeal & almond cake (crumble cake)

scalogno (i), shallot

scaloppa, veal scallop (thin slices of veal)

scaloppa alla fiorentina, veal scallop w/spinach & white sauce

scaloppa milanese, breaded, fried veal scallop

scaloppa napoletana, veal scallop coated in breadcrumbs

scaloppina (e), veal scallop

scaloppine alla boscaiola, veal scallops sautéed in oil & butter
  & served w/an herb, black olive & onion sauce

scaloppine alla campagnola, veal scallops served in a sauce.
  The term means "rustic"

scaloppine al marsala, small veal scallops in marsala wine

scaloppine al vino bianco, small veal scallops in
  white-wine sauce

scamorza, mild cheese (aged *mozzarella*)

scampi, shrimp/prawns

scampi all'Americana, shrimp in a tomato sauce

scanello, sirloin

scapece, fried fish in vinegar & saffron/fried vegetables which
  are then marinated

scarda, bream (fish)

scarola, escarole (a crispy leaf lettuce)

scarpaccia, zucchini pie (means "old shoe")

scarpena, scorpion fish

scelta, of your choice

schiacciata, flat bread (means "squashed flat")

schila, shrimp in Venice

schmarren, crêpes w/fruit & cream from Trentino-Alto Adige

scialatielli, wide noodles

scialcione, bread loaf

sciroppato (a), cooked in syrup

sciroppo, syrup

sciroppo d'acero, maple syrup

scodella, bowl

scorfano, scorpion fish

scorfano rosso, scorpion fish

scodella.

scorze d'amelle, pasta shaped like slivered almonds found in
Basilicata

scorzonera, salsify

scotch, scotch

scottadito, grilled lamb chops

scottiglia di cinghiale, wild-boar chops

scrippelle, omelettes cut into thin strips & served in a meat
broth. A specialty in Abruzzo & Molise

sebadas, bread filled w/cheese & honey, then fried.
A Sardinian specialty

secco (a), dry. *Funghi secchi* are dried mushrooms

secondo piatto, second course

sedani, the name for a small pasta similar to *rigatoni*

sedano, celery

sedano rapa, celery root

segale, rye

sella, saddle

selvaggina, game/venison

semente/semenza/senze, seeds

semi di, seeds of...

semi di melone, pasta noodle for soup in the shape of
melon seeds

semifreddi, (half-cold) desserts frozen or refrigerated
before service

semigreggio integrale, semi-whole wheat rice

semolino, flour

semplice, plain
senape, mustard
senza, without
seppia (e), cuttlefish/squid
seppioline, small cuttlefish/squid
serpentone, pastry stuffed w/chopped figs, apples & nuts
servizio, service/service charge
servizio compreso, service included
servizio incluso, service included
servizio non compreso, service not included
servizio non incluso, service not included
sesamo, sesame
sete, thirsty
sevàdas, Sardinian deep-fried pastries
sfilatino, bread loaf
sfogie, Venetian word for sole
sfoglia/sfogliatella/sfogliatelli, flaky-crusted shell-shaped
    pastry filled w/sweetened *ricotta* cheese
sfogliata, flaky pastry
sfogliata di crema, cream puff
sformato, similar to a souffle
sfratti, sweet walnut rolls (a Christmas dessert)
sgavecio, pickled fish
sgombro (i), mackerel
sidro, cider
sigarette, cigarettes
silvano, chocolate tart
Silvestro, herb & mint liqueur
smacafam, *polenta* dish w/*asiago*
    cheese & sausage

Smacafam means hunger killer

Soave, slightly dry white wine from Veneto
sodo/sode, hard boiled
soffritto, sautéed/stock (the base for soup or the sauce for
    pasta) often made w/pigs' organs. Can also refer to slightly
    fried or browned onions, carrots & celery, a base for many
    dishes
sogliola, sole   *Sogliola SO-LEE-OH LA*
sogliola all'Arlecchino, sole served w/a cream sauce
sogliola alla mugnaia, sole sautéed w/lemon, butter & parsley
sogliola margherita, sole covered w/hollandaise sauce
soia, soy
sopa, soup

sopa cauda, soup w/bread & roast pigeon
soppressa, sausage
soppressata, sausage/sausage made from pig's head
sorbetto, sherbet/sorbet
sorbetto al calvados, sherbet flavored w/apple brandy
sorrentina, often refers to a tomato, basil & mozzarella sauce
sottaceti, pickles
sottaceto, pickled
sottoaceti, pickled vegetables/pickles
sottofiletto, beef or veal loin
sott'olio, in olive oil
sottonoce, top round of veal
spaccatina, bread loaf
spaghetti, spaghetti (long, thin pasta)
spaghetti aglio e olio, spaghetti w/olive oil & garlic
spaghetti alla bolognese, spaghetti w/meat sauce
spaghetti alla carbonara, spaghetti w/cream, bacon,
  cheese & egg
spaghetti alla checca, spaghetti w/raw tomatoes, basil & garlic
spaghetti alla gricia, spaghetti w/onions, bacon, pepper &
  grated cheese
spaghetti all'amatriciana, w/tomato sauce, cheese & garlic
spaghetti alle vongole, spaghetti w/clam sauce
spaghetti al ragù, pasta w/meat & tomato sauce
spaghettini, thin spaghetti
spaghetti pomodoro e basilico, spaghetti w/tomatoes & basil
spalla, shoulder
spanocci, very large prawns
sparaci, asparagus in Venice
sparnocci, type of shrimp
specialità della casa, specialty of the house
specialità di questa regione, specialty of the region
specialità di questo ristorante, specialty of the restaurant
specialità locali, local specialties
specialità regionali, regional specialties/local dishes
speck, cured ham found in the Trentino-Alto Adige region
spelt, a hard wheat
speziato, spicy
spezie, spice
spezzatino, meat or poultry stew/little pieces
spezzato, a stew
spicchio (d'aglio), clove (of garlic)

Sotto aceti means under vinegar (handwritten)

spiedini alla corsara flambe, grilled meat served "flaming"

spiedini di mare, pieces of grilled fish on a skewer

spiedino (i), any dish roasted on a skewer

spiedo, allo, on a spit

spiga di grano, ear of corn

spigola, sea bass/grouper

spinaci, spinach

spiza di grano, ear of corn

spremuta, fresh fruit drink

spugnola, morel mushroom

spuma, mousse

spumante, sparkling wine

spumone (i), ice cream w/candied fruit, nuts & whipped cream

spumoni al croccante, *spumoni* topped w/toasted, caramelized almonds

spuntatura, breast of...

spuntino, snack

stagionato (a), well aged

stagione (i), season (in season)

starna, a type of partridge

stecca di, bar of

stecchi fritti, fried kebabs

stecchino, toothpick/skewer

stellette/stelline, star-shaped pasta

stinchetti, marzipan cakes (in the shape of human bones)

stinco, braised veal or pork shank. The most common version of this dish is ***stinco di maiale al forno***, a whole pork shank oven-roasted w/wine, garlic & rosemary

Stinco actually means shin bone.

stoccafisso, dried cod

storione, sturgeon

stracchino, a soft, creamy white cheese

stracciate, scrambled eggs

stracciatella, egg-drop soup. This can also refer to chocolate-chip ice cream

stracotto, beef stew w/pork sausage/ pot roast

strangolapreti, see *strozzapreti*

strangozze, see *stringozzi*

strapazzate, scrambled

strascinati, shell-shaped pasta

stravecchio, *parmesan* cheese aged at least three years

Strega, a strong herb liqueur

strigghie, red mullet in Sicily

stringozzi, a homemade pasta from Umbria

strisce, ribbon noodles

strozzapreti, dumplings or *gnocchi* w/meat sauce.

Strozzapreti means Priest stranglers. A gluttonous priest supposedly choked to death on one.

strudel, this famous pastry roll can be found in Trentino-Alto Adige

strutto, lard

stufatino, pot roast or stew

stufato, braised/stewed/stew

stuzzicadenti, toothpicks

stuzzichino (i), appetizer

succhi di frutta, sweetened fruit juice

succo, juice

succo di frutta, fruit juice

succu tunnu, dumpling soup

Succu tunnu. Never had it but love the name.

sufflé, soufflé

sugna, lard

sugna piccante, a spicy sauce made from pork fat (added to dishes in Basilicata)

sugo, sauce/gravy/juice

sugo, al, w/tomato sauce

suino, pork

suppli/suppli di riso, breaded & deep-fried rice balls usually filled w/ham & cheese

suprema di pollo in gelatina, chicken breast in aspic

suro, mackerel

susina (e), plum

tacchino, turkey

tacchino TA-KEE-NO

tagliata di manzo, grilled beef

tagliatelle, short ribbon noodles

taglierini, thin noodles

taglierini alla chitarra, a pasta dish featuring a sheet of pasta cut w/a cutter called a *"chitarra"* or guitar

tagliolini, very narrow, thin flat noodles

tajarin, egg noodles found in Piedmont & Valle d'Aosta

taleggio, cheese w/a mild, buttery flavor

taralli, biscuits made in the shape of a ring

tartara, alla, raw w/lemon sauce

tartaruga, turtle

tartina (e), open-faced sandwich/tart.
  Tartine are often appetizers
tartufi di cioccolato, chocolate "truffles"
  (chocolate-coated ice cream)
tartufi di mare, small clams/cockles
tartufo (i), truffle (funghi that grows around tree trunks)
tartufo di gelato, ice cream w/chocolate sauce
tartufo nero, black truffle from Tuscany
tasse, taxes. Menus will often indicate if *tasse e servizio* (taxes
  & service) are included
tavola (o), table
tavola calda, snack bar/fast food
tavoletta di cioccolata, chocolate bar
tazza, cup
tè, tea
tè cinese, Chinese tea
tè d'India, Indian tea
tè freddo, iced tea
tegamaccio, lake-fish stew from Umbria
tegame/tegamino, al, sautéed
teglia, alla, pan-fried
teglia di pesce spada, marinated swordfish dish
tellina (e), clam
teneroni, veal chops
terrina, tureen
testa, head. *Testa di vitello* is calf's head *I'll pass.*
testina, head
testuggine, turtle
tiedde, fish casserole from Apulia
tiella, any dish with baked layers of ingredients
tiella di agnello, roasted lamb dish
tiella di riso e cozze, mussels, rice & potato dish found in
  Apulia
tigelle, flat bread
timbale/timballo, meat & vegetable casserole w/layers of pasta
timo, thyme
tinca (tinche), tench (seafood)
tiramisù, spongecake soaked in
  espresso & brandy w/cream &
  chocolate. *Marsala* can also
  be used in this
  delicious dessert

TAZZA di tè.

Tira misu made its way to Italy from the U.S.

tirolese, alla, usually means w/fried onion rings

tisana, herbal tea

tisana al cinorrode, rose-hip tea

tisana al tiglio, lime tea

tisana camomilla, camomile tea

tocco di funghi, mushroom sauce

toc de purcit, pork stew w/white wine from Friuli-Venezia Giulia

toma, sharp cheese

tomini, fresh cheese from Piedmont

tonarelli/tonarrelli/tonnarelli, thin string pasta

tondino, bread loaf

tonica, tonic water

tonnato, in a tuna sauce. Can also refer to a cold veal dish

tonnetto, small tuna

tonno, tuna

topinambur, artichoke (Jerusalem artichoke)

tordo (i), thrush (a bird)

torlo, yolk

torrone, nougat

torta (e), tort/cake/pie

Torrone is immensely popular in Italy.

torta al pesto, spinach & cheese pie/flat bread cooked over hot stones in Umbria & filled w/cheese, meat or greens

torta di frutta, fruit tart

torta di gelato, ice-cream cake — yes please.

torta di mele, apple tart

torta di tagliatelle, egg-noodle cake

torta di verdure, sweet vegetable pie (similar to American pumpkin pie)

torta gianduia, chocolate & nut cake

torta meringa, large meringue pie filled w/fruit & topped w/whipped cream

torta millefoglie, napoleon (layers of pastry filled w/ice cream or whipped cream & topped w/frosting)

torta Pasqualina, Easter puff-pastry cake

torta rustica, cornmeal-cake dessert

torta sbrisolona, flour, cornmeal & almond cake (crumble cake)

torta tarantina, potato pie

torta turchesca, rice-pudding tart from Venice

torta zuccotto, liquor-soaked sponge cake filled w/ice
cream or whipped cream, chocolate & candied fruits

tortelli di zucca, pasta stuffed w/pumpkin

tortellini, filled pasta rings

tortello (i), small doughnut/fritter

tortellone (i), a larger *tortellini* pasta

tortiera, cake/pie

tortiglione, almond cakes

tortiglioni, tube-shaped pasta (larger than *cannelloni*)

tortina di marmellata, jam tart

tortini di riso, rice cakes

tortino, tart/cheese & vegetable tart similar to quiche

tortino di carciofi, dish of fried artichokes & eggs

toscana, alla, w/tomatoes & herbs

tostato (a), toasted

totano (i), squid

tournedos, small tenderloin steaks

tovaglia, table cloth

tovagliolo, napkin

Tovagliolo

TOV - A - LEE - OH - LO

tozzetti, hazelnut & almond biscuits (flavored w/anise)

tracina dragone, a fish named "dragon" after its
dangerous spines

tramezzino, small sandwich

trancia/trancio, piece/slice

trattaliu, cooked lamb intestines. A specialty in Sardinia

trenette, long, flat, thin ribbon noodles

trifolati, sliced mushrooms cooked in butter, garlic & oil

trifolato, w/truffles

triglia (e), red mullet

triglia alla Livornese, red mullet cooked w/tomatoes, garlic &
parsley

trigoli, water chestnuts

trippa (e), tripe

trippa alla fiorentina, braised
tripe & minced beef
w/tomato sauce & cheese

trippa alla milanese, tripe
w/onions, carrots, tomatoes,
beans & leeks

trippa alla romana, tripe in a
tomato & vegetable sauce

You can put all the "ALLA"s you want on trippa and it's still TRIPE.

tritato (a), ground (as in ground beef)

trofie, pasta similar to *gnocchi*

trombetta da morto, a type of mushroom

trota (e), trout

trota alle mandorle, stuffed-trout dish

trota di ruscello, river trout

trota iridea, rainbow trout

trota salmonata, salmon trout

trota spaccata, trout split in two, dipped in batter & deep-fried

trotella, trout

tuaca, a mixture of brandy, citrus fruits & herbs

tubetti, *macaroni*

tubi, refers to all tubular pasta

tuorlo, yolk

tutto compreso, all included

ua, grapes in Venice

ubriaco, cooked in red wine

uccelletti/uccelli, small birds (of
all kinds) usually spit-roasted

uccelletto, all', w/tomato sauce & sage. *Piselli all' uccelleto*
are peas cooked in tomato sauce w/sage

uccelli scappati, pork, pork sausage &/or small-bird kebabs

ueta, raisin in Venice

uliva, olive

umido, in, stewed

uopa, sea bream

uova, eggs

uova affogate, poached eggs

uova affogate nel vino, eggs poached in wine

uova à la coque, soft-boiled eggs

uova albume, egg whites

uova al burro, eggs fried in butter

uova al guscio, soft-boiled eggs

uova alla campagnola, eggs w/diced vegetables & cheese

uova alla coque, boiled eggs

uova alla fiorentina, fried eggs served on spinach

uova all'americana, fried eggs (usually served w/bacon)

uova alla russa, similar to deviled eggs

uova all'occhio di bue, fried eggs

uova al tegame con formaggio, fried eggs w/cheese

uova barrotte, soft-boiled eggs

uova bollite, soft-boiled eggs

uova frittata/uova fritte, fried omelette
uova frittata al pomodoro, tomato omelette
uova frittata al prosciutto, ham omelette
uova in camicia, poached eggs
uova molli/uova mollette, soft-boiled eggs
uova ripiene, stuffed eggs
uova semplice, plain omelette
uova sode agli spinaci, eggs florentine
uova tonnate, hard-boiled eggs in tuna sauce
uovo (a), egg
uovo fritto (uova fritte), fried egg
uovo sodo (uova sode), hard-boiled egg
uovo strapazzatto (uova strapazzate), scrambled egg
uva, grapes
uva bianca, green grapes
uva nera, black grapes
uva passa/uva passita, raisins
uva secca, raisin
uva spina, gooseberry
uvetta, white raisins
vaniglia, vanilla
valdostana, alla, usually means served w/ham & cheese
    (means "Valle d'Aosta style")
valigetta, roasted veal breast
Valpolicella, light (slightly bitter) red wine from Veneto
vapore, a, steamed
vario/vari, assorted
Vecchia Romagna, wine-distilled brandy
vegetable, vegetable
vegetariano (a), vegetarian
velluta, creamy soup
veneziana, alla, w/onions, white wine & sometimes mint
ventaglio, scallop
ventresca, white-meat tuna. Can also mean a boiled pork dish
verde, green/green pasta (w/a spinach base)
verde in pinzimonio, vegetable dip
Verdicchio, a dry white wine from Le Marche
verdura (e), green vegetable
verdura trovata, sautéed wild greens w/potatoes
verdure cotte, cooked vegetables
vermicelli, thin, long spaghetti noodles
vermut, vermouth

verza, cabbage

verzelata, grey mullet

vincigrassi/vincisgrassi, baked lasagna dish. Named after an Austrian prince, this dish is a specialty in the region of Le Marche where it's usually served w/chicken-giblet sauce

vincotto, a spread made from grapes

vinello, light wine

vino (i), wine

vino amabile, sweet wine

vino asciutto, very dry wine

vino bianco, white wine

vino brut, very dry wine

vino corposo, full-bodied wine

vino da pasto, table wine

vino da tavola, table wine (the lowest-quality wine made from any combination of grapes)

vino del paese, local wine

vino dolce, sweet wine

vino frizzante, sparkling wine

vino leggero, light wine

vino nostrano, local wine

vino novello, new wine

vino rosatello, rosé wine

vino rosato, rosé wine

vino rosé, rosé (blush) wine

vino roseo, rosé wine

vino rosso, red wine

Vin Santo/Vinsanto, dessert wine from Tuscany & Trentino

vino secco, dry wine

vino semi secco, semi-sweet wine

vino spumante, sparkling wine

vino tipico, local wine

violino, cured leg of goat

visciola, wild cherry

vitellini, very young veal

vitello, veal

vitello all'uccelletto, diced veal & sage simmered in wine

vitello tonnato, cold veal w/tuna sauce

vodka, vodka

vol-au-vents, filled pastry shells

vongola (e), small clam

amabile also means loveable which pretty much refers to all wine as far as we're concerned.

vino da tavola is low quality wine but not necessarily bad.

You weren't really looking this up were you?

vongole, alle, in a clam sauce

vongole oreganate, clams baked or broiled w/oregano

vongole veraci, small clams boiled in vinegar,
   hot pepper & garlic

whisky, whiskey

wurstel, hot dogs (similar to smoked hot dogs)

yogurt/yoghurt, yogurt

yogurt magro, low-calorie yogurt. *Yogurt intero* is not low-fat

zabaglione/zabaione, custard dessert flavored w/Marsala

zafferano, saffron

zalettini, shortbread cookies from Venice *I'll pass.*

zampa (e), pig's (or beef) feet

zampetto, pork leg

zampone, large pig's foot scraped clean of its insides & then
   stuffed w/spicy sausage

zampone di maiale, stuffed pigs' feet

zelten, dried fruit & nut cake from Trentino-Alto Adige

zenzero, ginger

zèppola, doughnut/fritter *— Si, grazie!*

zesti, orange or lemon peel (can also be candied)

ziba, fragrant herb from Sardinia

zimini, in, cooked w/vegetables. *In zimino* can refer to spinach
   or Swiss chard stewed w/cod or squid & tomatoes

zimino, Sardinian fish stew

zingara, alla, "Gypsy style." Each chef has his or her own
   version of this sauce of many ingredients

zite (i), narrow, hollow-tube pasta

zucca, pumpkin or squash

zucca ovifera, squash

zucchero, sugar

zucchero a velo, powdered sugar

zucchero a zollette, lump sugar

zucchero greggio, brown sugar

zucchero grezzo, brown sugar

zucchero in pezzi, lump sugar

zucchero in polvere, powdered sugar

Zuchine
zoo·KEEN·E

zucchine al burro versato, zucchini w/black-butter sauce

zucchine farcite, zucchini filled cheese, ham & mushrooms

zucchine fritte, deep-fried strips of zucchini

zucchine scapecce, pieces of zucchini fried in oil w/garlic

zucchine trifolate, sliced zucchini in butter, parsley & garlic

zucchino (i), zucchini

zucchina (e), zucchini
zuccotto, ice cream-filled cake
zuchette, zucchini
zuppa, soup
zuppa alla coltivatore, vegetable soup with diced bacon
zuppa alla pavese, soup w/croutons, grated cheese & poached egg
zuppa di arzilla, soup made w/ray fish & broccoli
zuppa di cereali, bean, vegetable & grain stew
zuppa di cipolle alla Francese, french onion soup
zuppa di cozze, mussel soup
zuppa di datteri, fish-soup specialty of Liguria
zuppa di fagioli, bean soup
zuppa di farro, soup made with *farro* (a wheat similar to spelt)
zuppa di frutti di mare, seafood soup
zuppa di lenticchie, lentil soup
zuppa di pesce, fish stew
zuppa di pollo, chicken soup
zuppa di telline, soup w/tiny clams
zuppa di verdura, vegetable soup
zuppa di vongole, clam soup w/white wine
zuppa d'orzo, barley & potato soup
zuppa fredda, cold soup
zuppa inglese, not a soup at all. Spongecake soaked in liquor w/cream filling & whipped cream
zuppa pavese, clear soup w/a poached egg
zuppa valdostana, cabbage soup from the Val d'Aosta region
zuppa di zucca, soup made from small squash or pumpkin

Zuppa di Farro.. love it.

Buon Appetito!

Phone numbers, days closed and hours of operation often change, so it's advisable to check ahead. Restaurants in tourist areas may have different hours and days of operation during low season. Reservations are recommended for all restaurants unless noted. The telephone country code for Italy is 39.

Prices are for main courses and without wine. Lunch, even at the most expensive restaurants listed below, always has a lower fixed price. Credit cards are accepted unless noted otherwise.

Inexpensive: under 10 euros
Moderate: 11 – 20 euros
Expensive: 21 – 30 euros
Very Expensive: over 30 euros

Amalfi Coast
Da Emilia
This eatery is located in an old boat shed near the Marina Grande in Sorrento. Try to score a table outside so you can watch the fishermen. The emphasis here is on Sorrentine cuisine, like *gnocchi alla Sorrentina* (potato dumplings with a simple tomato-and-cheese sauce). The grilled *calamari* is delicious. This isn't fine dining, but this family-owned place is a nice change from all the fancier restaurants that are prevalent on the Amalfi Coast. *Info*: 62 Via Marina Grande (Sorrento). Tel. 081/8072720. Closed Tue from Nov-Feb.
www.daemilia.it.
Inexpensive – Moderate.

We think, hope and pray that our restaurant list is current & correct, but remember... things change. Call first or do a "walk-by" in the afternoon. Stop in, make a reservation— they'll love you for it.

La Villa Ristobar
It's all about the view at this restaurant/bar/cafe located on
the Villa Comunale in Sorrento. Enjoy an *aperitif*, espresso,
or wine while you take in the Gulf of Naples, Mount
Vesuvius, and the island of Capri. If you want to snack, try
a *panino* (sandwich), pastry, or the delicious homemade ice
cream. *Info*: Piazza Francesco Saverio Gargiulo (Sorrento).
Tel. 081/8074090. Open daily. www.lavillasorrento.it.
Moderate.

Il Marzialino
This attractive steak house and wine bar is located in
the historical center of Sorrento, overlooking the Villa
Comunale (the largest public park in Sorrento on a cliff
overlooking the Bay of Naples). Featured dishes include
carpaccio con parmigiano e misticanza (raw Black Angus
beef with parmesan and a mixed-green salad) and *lombata
di vitello* (veal chop). You won't go home hungry if you
order one of the many steaks available. Save room for the
delicious *panna cotta* (rich cream custard). They have a
very good local wine selection. *Info*: 2 Largo F.S. Gargiulo
(Sorrento). Tel. 081/8074406. www.terrazzamarziale.com.
Moderate – Expensive.

La Caravella
Lovely restaurant in Amalfi known for its celebrity guests
and its seafood dishes, especially *calamari* (squid) and
polpo (octopus). The specialty here is *trito di pesce gri-
gliato in foglia di limone con erba finocchiella e mandorle*
(lemon leaves stuffed with finely shredded fish, grilled and
served with wild fennel sauce and almonds). The restaurant
is known for its extensive wine list, especially those from
the Campania region. *Info*: 12 Via Matteo Camera (Amalfi).
Tel. 089/871029. Closed Tue, most of Nov, and mid-Jan to
mid-Feb. www.ristorantelacaravella.it.
Expensive – Very Expensive.

Da Gemma
Specialties of Campania (especially seafood), with summer
dining on the terrace. Choices include the *zuppa di pesce*
(fish stew) for two, *tonno rosso arrostito con broccoli e
couscous* (grilled tuna served with broccoli and couscous),

and *filetto di manzo con carciofi e patate* (filet of beef with artichokes and potatoes). *Info*: 9 Via Frà Gerardo Sasso (Amalfi). Tel. 089/871345. Closed Wed and Jan to mid-Mar. www.trattoriadagemma.com. Expensive.

Da Aldolfo

After a five-minute boat ride, you'll arrive at Laurito beach where you'll find this beachfront restaurant and bar. There are changing rooms and showers, and you can rent an umbrella and lounge chair. The specialty here is grilled mozzarella on lemon leaves. Delicious fresh fish dishes, too. Unique! *Info*: 40 Via Laurito (Positano). Accessible by the "red fish" boat departing from the main pier from 10am-1pm and 4pm to about 6:30pm (later on Sat in Jul and Aug). Tel. 089/875022. Closed Oct - Apr. Reservations required. www.daadolfo.com. Moderate.

Cumpa' Cosimo

This family-owned restaurant in Ravello focuses on local dishes. One of the dishes is the simply named *misto*. It's a mix of seven different pastas topped with seven different sauces. Hope you're hungry! You can also order the *frittura di pesce* (fish fry) or meat dishes. *Info*: 44 Via Roma (Ravello). Tel. 089/857156. Closed Mon from Nov-Feb. Inexpensive – Moderate.

Assisi
Bibenda

This small, cozy *enoteca* (wine bar) with vaulted ceilings is a must-stop when visiting Assisi. Located on a street off of the Piazza del Comune, you'll be welcomed by sommelier Nila Halun. Wine tastings are offered and feature classic Umbrian wines paired with regional cheeses, homemade bread, *prosciutto* (aged and cured ham), *cinghale* (wild boar), and *cervo* (venison). If you're not interested in a wine tasting, take your pick from the wines by the glass. We enjoyed the "Degustazione Rosso di Assisi," a glass of local red wine paired with *capocollo* (smoked pork salami) for under €10. *Info*: 9 Via Nepis (near Via San Rufino), Tel. 075/8155176. Closed Tue. www.bibendaassisi.it. Inexpensive – Moderate.

La Fortezza

Traditional Umbrian dishes (including veal, duck, and rabbit). If you've never tried *coniglio* (rabbit), this is the place. It's roasted in a delicious sauce with apples and wine. Good food at reasonable prices served under vaulted brick ceilings. Also recommended is the *cannelloni all'Assisiana* (sheets of pasta wrapped around veal and baked under parmesan cheese). *Info*: 2B Vicolo della Fortezza (alley off of the Piazza del Comune). Tel. 075/812993. Closed Thu, Feb, and part of Jul. www.lafortezzaristorante.it. Moderate.

Medioevo

Located in the historic center of town, you'll dine under stone-vaulted ceilings. Try the excellent *scottadito di agnello* (grilled lamb chop) or the tasty *penne alla norcina* (penne in a sausage-and-cheese sauce). Good selection of Tuscan and Umbrian wines. *Info*: 4B Via dell'Arco dei Priori (near Piazza del Comune). Tel. 075/813068. Closed Mon. Dinner Tue-Fri, Sat lunch and dinner, Sun lunch only. www.ristorantemedioevoassisi.it. Moderate.

Osteria Piazzetta dell'Erba

When the weather is warm, you can sit outside and try the Assisi specialty *torta al testa* (flatbread stuffed with sausage, cheese, and/or vegetables). You can also dine inside under the vaulted brick ceiling surrounded by shelves filled with local wines. For dinner, try the *faraona* (guinea fowl) served in a port sauce with *frutti di bosco* (berries) or the grilled *polipo* (octopus). The wines here are from local vineyards and bottled by the restaurant. *Info*: 15a Via San Gabriele dell'Addolorata (near the Cattedrale di San Rufino). Tel. 075/815352. Closed Mon. www.osterialapiazzetta.it. Moderate.

Bergamo
Taverna del Colleoni dell'Angelo

The specialties of Lombardy and the Lake District served in a historic building in the heart of the Old Town. Excellent homemade ravioli. Outdoor dining in summer. *Info*: 7 Piazza Vecchia. Tel. 035/232596. Closed Mon. www.colleonidellangelo.com. Moderate – Expensive.

Caffè del Tasso

This café and restaurant is also on the Piazza Vecchia. Have an *aperitvo* (aperitif) served with home-baked cookies, or have a light lunch. Very good salads. Try the *polentina con salsiccia e funghi porcini* (*polenta* with sausage and porcini mushrooms). The same owners run the *gelateria* next door where you can sample creamy and delicious ice cream. *Info*: 3 Piazza Vecchia. Tel. 035/237966. Open daily. Moderate.

Ristorante Lalimentari

This wine bar and restaurant is located in Bergamo Alta near Piazza Vecchia. Exposed stone and walls lined with wine bottles make this an attractive place to wine and dine. For a first plate, try *casoncelli alla bergamasca* (pasta stuffed with ground meat and cooked in a butter, bacon, and sage sauce). There are several *polenta* dishes on the menu, including the rich *polenta taragna* (corn flour and buckwheat flour are boiled in water with salt, then three regional cheeses are added). The wine list features local wines like Valcalepio: *Valcalepio Rosso* is produced from a blend of Cabernet Sauvignon and Merlot, and *Valcalepio Bianco* is a blend of Pinot Bianco Chardonnay, and Pinot Grigio. Try some! *Info*: 3A Via Tassis. Tel. 035/233043. Closed Mon. www.lalimentari.it. Moderate.

Pasticceria Nessi

Open since 1946, this *pasticceria* (pastry shop) is the place to try the Bergamo specialty *polenta e osei*. It's a light spongecake filled with hazelnut cream that is rolled in a yellow fondant and topped with "baby birds" made from chocolate marzipan. You'll see locals and tourists peering at the window displays. *Info*: 34 Via Gombito. Tel. 035/247073.

Bologna

Tamburini

This lively place in the city center has been in business since 1932. Locals jam the small eatery to sample pasta dishes. After lunch, it turns into a wine bar. Excellent *affettati misti* (plate of cold cuts and cheese). Great selection of local wines by the glass. Its food shop sells interesting local wine and food specialties. *Info*: 1 Via Caprarie (at Via Calzolerie). Tel. 051/234726. Open daily. www.tamburini.com. Inexpensive – Moderate.

Drogheria della Rosa

This friendly *trattoria* with an extensive wine cellar is located in a former pharmacy. The chef presides over this lovely mess of a place. There is no written menu. We had the best *lasagne bolognese* here. Don't leave without trying the tortelli stuffed with zucchini blossoms. Bologna is the gastronomic capital of Italy, and this place shows you why. *Info*: 10 Via Cartoleria (at Via Dè Choari). Tel. 051/222529. Closed Sun and part of Aug. www.drogheriadellarosa.it. Moderate – Expensive.

Da Cesari

Romantic restaurant with wood-panelled walls, serving delicious Bolognese dishes. Try the *scaloppa di vitello*. The Cesari family has presided over the restaurant since the 1950s. You should try the house specialty, flavorful pork called *mora romagnola*. *Info*: 8 Via de'Carbonesi (south of Piazza Maggiore). Tel. 051/237710. Closed Sun and most of Aug. www.da-cesari.it. Moderate – Expensive.

Enoteca Italiana

Deli, wine bar, and food-and-wine shop near the famous Neptune Fountain. Great place to stock up on local specialties and snacks for a picnic. They serve great sandwiches, and wine by the glass. *Info*: 2B Via Marsala (north of Piazza Maggiore). Tel. 051/235989. Closed Tue (except Nov and Dec). www.enotecaitaliana.it.

Cremeria Santo Stefano

You'll know when you've arrived at this ice-cream shop, as there is almost always a line to get served. Try the delicious salty pistachio! It's a little outside the city center, but certainly worth the walk. Good choice if you're traveling with children. The shop itself is quite attractive. *Info*: 70/c Via Santo Stefano (at via Remorsella). Tel. 051/227045. Open 10am-11:30pm. Closed Mon. www.facebook.com/CremeriaSantoStefano.

Osteria del Sole

In business since 1465, this fun (and often chaotic) wine bar is a great experience. No food is served here, but you can purchase sausage, ham, bread, and cheese from one of the nearby stores (or at the market) and bring it with you. Enjoy Italian wines by the glass (starting at €2) and by the bottle. *Info*: 1/d Vicolo Ranocchi (between Via degli Orefici and Via Pescherie Vecchie). Tel. 348/2256887. Open 10:30am-9:30pm. Closed Sun. www.osteriadelsole.it. Inexpensive.

La Tana dell'Orso

There's a warm welcome at this small, casual restaurant with red-checkered curtains. This family-run place is a bit out of the way, but worth the trip if you're watching your euros. Try the tasty *piadina* (soft flat-bread) topped with everything from *pancetta* (cured pork belly) to *salame* (smoked sausage). *Info*: 10/c Via Portazza (between Via Treviso and Via Vicenza). Tel. 051/465437. Open Mon-Sat noon-2:30pm and 6:30pm-10pm, Sun 7pm-10pm. Closed Wed. www.latanadellorso.net. Moderate.

Eataly

Eataly is a chain of stores specializing in Italian food and wines. You'll find everything Italian at the Bologna location, including pasta, beer, wine, meats, desserts, and vegetables. You can eat and drink at one of the restaurants, bars, and cafes. There's a *trattoria* on the top floor. We love the attached bookstore. *Info*: 19 Via degli Orafici. Tel. 051/0952820. Open Mon-Sat 9am-11:30pm, Sun 10am-11:30pm. www.eataly.it.

Bologna: Markets

Bologna has two main food markets. Filled with colorful vendors, fresh produce, stinky cheese, and hanging meats, it's really worth the trip to experience the sights and smells.

Mercato di Mezzo

Open daily 9am-midnight. 12 Via Clavature (off of the Piazza Maggiore). Tel. 051/228782.

Mercato della Erbe

Open Mon-Thu 7am tomidnight, Fri and Sat 7am-2am. Closed Sun and Nov-Feb. 25 Via Ugo Bassi near the Piazza Maggiore. Tel. 051/230186. www.mercatodelleerbe.it.

Bologna: Cooking Classes

The city is known as "Bologna the Fat" for good reason. This is *the* food city in Italy. What better way to experience the wonderful world of Bologna's cuisine than to attend a cooking school? There are interesting classes offered. Bologna Cooking School offers half day cooking classes where you prepare ragù alla Bolognese. They also offer tours of the sights of the city. For prices and reservations, check out www.bolognacookingschool.com.

Capri

Pulalli

This wine bar and restaurant has a fantastic location next to the clock tower. Not to be missed is the *risotto al limone* (lemon-flavored *risotto* served in a half lemon). *Info*: 4 Piazza Umberto I. Tel. 081/8374108. Closed Tue and Nov to Easter. www.capri.com/en/c/pulalli-wine-bar. Moderate – Expensive.

Le Grottelle

It's worth the hike for the fabulous views from this rustic eatery. Try the *ravioli Capri* (ravioli filled with fresh cheese) or the *pasta con gamberetti e rucola* (pasta with shrimp and arugula). Top off your meal with a glass of *limoncello*. *Info*: 13 Via Arco Naturale. Tel. 081/8375719. Closed Thu. (except Jul-Sep) and mid-Nov to Mar. Moderate – Expensive.

Terrazza Brunella

Our friends are return visitors to the Villa Brunella, a boutique hotel in Capri. The restaurant at the hotel, perfect for a romantic lunch or dinner, is lovely at sunset with its view of the boats in the Marina Piccola. The food is as good as the view. Dishes include *ravioli capresi* (homemade pasta filled with cheese and fresh marjoram), and *salmone al vapore con patate al profumo zafferano* (steamed salmon with potatoes flavored with saffron). *Info*: 24 Via Tragara. Tel. 081/8370122. Open from Easter to the beginning of Nov. www.terrazzabrunella.com. Expensive.

Da Gelsomina

This unique complex has a guest house, restaurant (with a fabulous terrace), and swimming pool. It's located in a remote area of the island near the Belvedere della Migliera, one of Capri's cliffside viewing points. The restaurant sends its small buses to pick you up at the taxi stop down the road, and it's a lovely scenic ride. The pool and snack bar are open to the public, so you may want to come during the day and lounge about. The restaurant serves its own wine and has a long list of wines from the Campania region. Specialties include *coniglio* (rabbit) served in a mushroom, wine, and herb sauce, and *ravioli capresi* (ravioli with tomatoes, *mozzarella* and basil). *Info*: 72 Via Migliera (Anacapri). Tel. 081/8371499. Open daily. www.dagelsomina.com. Expensive.

Lido del Faro

Another place in Capri to watch the sunset. This gourmet restaurant and beach club can be your destination for the day. You can swim in the sun from dawn until dusk in the crystal-clear water, and then have dinner at the restaurant while the sun sets. The restaurant features fresh fish dishes. Specialties include *polipetti affogati con le olive* (octopus in an olive sauce), *ricciola con pesto alla menta* (sea urchin with mint pesto), and *ravioli con fiori di zucca e vongole* (clam-and-zucchini flower ravioli). A unique venue near the Grotta Azzurra (Blue Grotto). *Info*: Punta Carena (Anacapri). Tel. 081/8371798. Restaurant open daily noon to sunset from Easter to late October. Pool open from dawn to dusk. www.lidofaro.com.
Restaurant: Expensive.

Capri Pasta

On an island as expensive as Capri, this is a great alternative if you're watching your euros. The take-out food is excellent, and its location near Capri Town's main square is convenient. Choices include *polpettine al vino bianco* (meatballs in a white-wine sauce), *insalata di polpo* (octopus salad), and *ravioli fritti* (fried ravioli). *Info*: 12 Via Parroco Roberto Canale. Tel. 081/8370147. Open daily. Closed Jan and Feb. www.capripasta.com. Inexpensive.

The **Chiantigiana** (SR 222) runs from Florence to Siena through vineyards producing Chianti Classico, specifically Chianti Classico DOCG (the highest classification of Chianti).

Even if you're not a wine connoisseur, this route is worth the trip. You'll pass beautiful vineyards with ripening Sangiovese grapes and olives, scenic rolling hills, castles, abbeys and churches, and charming Tuscan towns. The trip is especially fun at harvest time (September) when many small towns hold wine festivals.

Most of the vineyards along the way are open to the public and have signs inviting you to visit. Look for signs offering *degustazioni* (tastings) and *vendita diretta* (direct sales). Here are just a few towns and wineries that you can visit along the way:

Castello di Verrazzano

They've been producing wine here since the 1100s! You can sample the specialty here (for free), Sassello, made from the Sangiovese grape. *Info*: 32A Via Citille (Greti). Tel. 055/855243. Open daily 10am-6pm. www.verrazzano.com.

Greve in Chianti

The small market town of Chianti, big on wine shops, should not be missed. Head to the triangular-shaped Piazza Matteotti. Not to be missed is the **Enoteca del Chianti Classico Gallo Nero**, which has been in business since 1969. *Info*: 8 Piazzetta S. Croce. Tel. 055/853297. Open daily from 9:30am-7:30pm Apr-Oct. Closed Wed Nov-Feb. www.chianticlassico.it.

Villa Vignamaggio

This villa, just south of Greve, dates back to the 1400s, and the winery produces Chianti Classico, Chianti Classico Riserva, and Vinsanto del Chianti Classico. If you book ahead, you can take part in a guided tour of the gardens and wine cellar, including a wine tasting and lunch. The shop is open daily, and has free wine and olive oil tastings. Oh, by the way, it is here that the woman who posed for da Vinci's "Mona Lisa" was born. *Info*: 5 Via Petriolo. Tel. 055/854661. Shop open daily 10:30am-6:30pm. www.vignamaggio.com.

Panzano in Chianti
You'll see the castle's tower on the hill as you approach lovely Panzano. You'll have great views of the countryside. The heart of the town is the triangular Piazza Bucciarelli, where you'll find many shops selling wine and the local embroidery.

Radda in Chianti
This small, attractive village is another center of the wine trade. Stroll the covered walkway that circles the city inside the medieval walls.

Nearby is **Castello di Volpaia**. It's not only a wine estate, but also a small village with accommodations, dining, and (of course) wine shops. You can tour the winery and taste its wines and olive oils in an attractive shop located in the tower. Unique! *Info*: 4 miles north of Radda in Chianti. Tel. 0577/738066. Open daily. Closed winter. www.volpaia.com.

Castellina in Chianti
You won't soon forget Castellina's panoramic views. The town is surrounded by 15th-century walls, and features a 15th-century palace on its main square. You'll also find several restaurants, wine shops, and hotels, making the town a great place to use as your base as you explore the surrounding area.

Cinque Terre
Vernazza Winexperience
This wine bar in Vernazza is a must for wine lovers visiting the Cinque Terre. Not only will you enjoy interesting local wines, but you'll do it while on the patio enjoying an incredible and breathtaking view of the sea. This is the place to be at sunset. Try a glass of wine for €5 or three wines for €10 (including olives, anchovies, and cheese). You can also order a cheese-and-meat platter and other light plates. If you want to taste interesting wines from around Cinque Terre, this is the place to visit. Your host is the charming Alessandro who speaks English and knows his Italian wines. His family has been in

Vernazza for over six generations. Part of the experience is finding the place. From the main square, walk up the stairs by Gianni Franzi at Via Guidoni, take a left up the steep staircase at Via S. Giovanni Battista, and look for the posters advertising the Winexperience. Ask for help if you get lost! *Info*: 41 Via San Giovanni Battista, Vernazza. Tel. 331/3433801. Open 5pm-9pm. Closed Nov-Mar. www.cinqueterrewinetasting.com. Inexpensive-Moderate.

De Mananan

Hearty fare served in the cellar of a home in the smallest Cinque Terre town. Many dishes feature *pesto*. Try the *pansoti* (triangular-shaped filled pasta). The house special-ty is *coniglio* (rabbit) served in a tasty white wine sauce. *Info*: 117 Via Fieschi, Corniglia. Tel. 0187/821166. Closed Tue, Nov, and part of Jan and Feb. Moderate – Expensive.

Marina Piccola

Dine on delicious *cozze* (mussels) or *zuppe di pesce* (fish stew) at this waterside restaurant. Fabulous views from the terrace at this hotel restaurant. *Info*: 120 Via Birolli/16 Via Lo Scalo, Manarola. Tel. 0187/920923. Closed Tue. www.hotelmarinapiccola.com. Moderate.

Miky

Ligurian seafood, baked in a wood-burning stove, served in this charming Cinque Terre town. Enjoy delicious *antipasti* while you take in the sea view. Do not miss the grilled *calamari*! *Info*: 104 Via Fegina, Monterosso al Mare. Tel. 0187/817608. Closed Tue from Sep to Jul, and all of Nov and Dec. www.ristorantemiky.it. Moderate – Expensive. Just a few doors down is the more casual **Catina di Miky**, a popular evening gathering place.

Gambero Rosso

Ligurian specialties at this harborside restaurant (it's been open for over 100 years). The creamy *pesto* is fantastic. End your dinner with a glass of *Sciacchetrà*, a local dessert wine. *Info*: 7 Piazza Marconi, Vernazza. Tel. 0187/812265. Closed Thu and mid-Dec to Mar. www.ristorantegamberorosso.net. Moderate – Expensive.

Belforte

You'll pay for the view at this interesting restaurant located in a medieval tower overlooking the sea. The view won't disappoint and neither will the local specialties served here. Reservations are essential, especially if you want to dine at sunset. Start with the *insalada di polpo* (octopus salad), and you can't go wrong ordering the excellent mixed grill seafood platter. *Info*: 42 Via Guidoni, Vernazza. Tel. 0187/812222. Closed Tue and Nov-Easter. www.ristorantebelforte.it. Very Expensive.

Enoteca Internazionale

This wine bar in Monterosso al Mare is located on the main drag of the *centro storico* (historic center). Sit under one of the umbrellas on the patio and try a local wine from little-known, artisanal producers. The wine bar also features a selection of over 500 wines from all regions of Italy and around the world. You can order snacks to go with your wine (cold cuts, cheese, anchovies, and *bruschetta*). And if you're spending some time in town, you might want to sign up for one of the wine tastings. *Info*: 62 Via Roma, Monterosso al Mare. Tel. 0187/817278. Closed Tue and Jan-Mar. www.enotecainternazionale.com.

Florence   *See Florence maps pages 152 and 153*

Buca Lapi

This restaurant is in a cellar under the Palazzo Antinori. Try the scampi giganti alla griglia (large grilled shrimp) under the vaulted ceiling, surrounded by old travel posters. The Florentine specialty *bistecca alla fiorentina* served here is a large, grilled T-bone steak, served rare. You might want to start your dinner with a bowl of *ribollita* (which means "reboiled"), a famous Tuscan soup made with bread and vegetables. There are many variations but the main ingredients always include leftover bread, beans, and vegetables such as carrots and cabbage. *Info*: 1r Via del Trebbio (at Via dei Tornabuoni). Tel. 055/213768. Closed Sun and part of Aug. No lunch. www.bucalapi.com. Expensive.

Casa del Vino

This small, friendly, and attractive wine bar and wine shop serves cheese, sausage, ham, cured meat, and sandwiches. Good selection of wines by the glass, especially wines from Tuscany. The staff will also help you pick out a bottle to drink in your hotel room or to take home. *Info*: 16/r Via dell'Ariento (off of Via Sant'Antonino). Tel. 055/215609. Closed Sun and part of Aug. Inexpensive.

Il Cibrèo and Cibreino

Florentine cuisine at this famous, attractive, and popular restaurant and *trattoria*. Try the *sformato* (souffle). This is the place to sample the traditional Tuscan specialty of *trippa* (tripe). The lively *trattoria* (Cibreino) shares a kitchen with the restaurant and is less expensive (note that the *trattoria* does not take reservations or credit cards). *Info*: Restaurant: 8r Via Verrocchio (off of Via de' Macci), Trattoria: 122r Via de' Macci, Caffè: 5r Via Verrocchio. Tel. 055/2341100 (restaurant). Closed Mon and part of Aug. www.cibreo.com. Moderate (*trattoria*) – Expensive (restaurant).

Coquinarius

This intimate, casual restaurant is located on a small street near the Duomo. A wide selection of reasonably priced salads and entrees make it a great choice for lunch. Try the pear and pecorino ravioli. They are known for their *carpaccio* (thinly sliced raw beef). You can also order wild boar, salmon, and octopus *carpaccio*. Lots of tourists. *Info*: 15/r Via dell'Oche. Tel. 055/2302153. Open daily. www.coquinarius.com. Moderate.

Enoteca Pitti Gola e Cantina

This warm and friendly *enoteca* (wine bar) is located opposite the Pitti Palace. A great choice for lunch or dinner when in the Oltrarno (the neighborhood south of the Arno River). It's just a short walk from the Ponte Vecchio. You need to book in advance, especially for dinner, since there are only six tables. Two brothers and a friend run the place, where the emphasis is on wines from Tuscany. They have an excellent selection of wines from Chianti. You can choose fresh pasta dishes, local cheese, and *salumi*. If you plan ahead, you can book a dinner with the owners (Fri and Sat) or a wine-tasting lunch. *Info*: 16 Piazza Pitti. Tel. 055/212704. Open 1pm to midnight. Closed Tue. www.pittigolaecantina.com. Moderate.

Frescobaldi Wine Bar
Small, attractive wine bar and restaurant with excellent
pasta dishes and a wide selection of wines by the glass. Try
the *piatto di gran salumi Toscani* (assorted Tuscan sala-
mis). Main dishes include *carrè di agnello* (rack of lamb)
and *involtini di vitella ripiena di zucchine e prosciutto* (veal
roll stuffed with zucchini and cured ham). The Frescobaldis
have owned a vineyard for over 700 years. *Info*: 2-4r Via
dei Magazzini (between Piazza della Signoria and Via d.
Condotta). Tel. 055/284724. Open daily.
www.deifrescobaldi.it. Moderate – Expensive.

Mario
This eatery near San Lorenzo and the Mercato Centrale has
been in business for over sixty years. Simple traditional
Florentine dishes are served at communal tables. Start with
zuppa di fagioli (bean soup), and for your main course try
peposo di manzo (beef stew), *tagliata di manzo al rosmarino* (boneless beefsteak with rosemary), or the tasty *bistecca
di maiale* (pork chop). *Info*: 2R Via Rosina (at the Piazza
Mercato Centrale). Tel. 055/218550. Open noon-3:30pm.
No dinner. Closed Sun and Aug. No reservations.
www.trattoriamario.com. Inexpensive – Moderate.

Trattoria Le Mossacce
Dine with locals and tourists on Florentine cuisine at reasonable prices. The restaurant has been around since the
early 1900s. Florentine favorites such as *ossobuco* (braised
veal shank), *trippa* (tripe), and *ribollita* (vegetable soup
thickened with bread) are featured here. This is not fine
dining. Dishes are simple, and the house wine is a decent
Chianti. Info: 55r Via del Proconsolo (near Piazza del
Duomo). *Tel*. 055/294361. Closed Sat, Sun and Aug. No
reservations. www.trattorialemossacce.it. Inexpensive –
Moderate.

Trattoria La Casalinga
This unassuming trattoria is located near the church of
Santo Spirito south of the River Arno. The name means
"housewife," and you'll find Tuscan specialties here.
Tables are quite close together, where you'll dine with a
mixture of tourists and locals. It's known for its *ribollita*

(vegetable soup thickened with bread) and for its decent pasta dishes such as *pasta Bolognese*. Try the *coniglio al forno* (baked rabbit) for something different. *Info*: 9/r Via Michelozzi. Tel. 055/218624. Closed Sun and part of Aug. www.trattorialacasalinga.it. Inexpensive – Moderate.

Le Volpi e l'Uva

This *enoteca* (wine bar) is located south of the Arno River between the Ponte Vecchio and the Pitti Palace. There is a good selection of the Italian and French wines from lesser-known wineries. You can also munch on an equally good selection of Italian and French cheese, cured meats, and *crostini*. *Info*: Piazza de'Rossi (off of Piazza Santa Felicita). Tel. 555/2398132. Open Mon-Sun 11am-9pm. Closed Sun. www.levolpieluva.com. Inexpensive – Moderate.

Florence: *Gelato*

Florence claims to be the birthplace of *gelato* (ice cream). That may or may not be true, but everyone in the city seems to have an opinion on the best place to have it. Here are a few suggestions.

Carapina

This *gelateria* (ice-cream shop) is known for its fruit flavors. Info: 18R Via Lambertesca, off of Via Por Santa Maria near the Ponte Vecchio. Also located on the Piazza Oberdan. Tel. 055/291128. www.carapina.it.

Il Procopio

Known for its interesting combination of flavors, the specialty here is "*La Follia*:" a *gelato* with caramelized figs, toasted almonds, and *Sachertorte* (the Austrian chocolate cake). Delicious! *Info*: 60R Via Pietrapiana (at Via dei Pepi). Tel. 555/2346014. Closed Mon.

Vivoli

This Florentine institution serves up some delicious flavors, everything from *fico* (fig) to *limoncini alla crema* (vanilla with lemon peels). *Info*: 7R Via Isola delle Stinche (a block west of Via G. Verdi, a backstreet near Piazza di Santa Croce). Tel. 055/292334. Closed Mon, Jan and Aug. No credit cards. www.vivoli.it. Inexpensive.

Florence: Food Shops
Vestri
Chocolate, chocolate, and more chocolate. Especially
good is the chocolate *gelato*. The attractively wrapped
chocolates, in pale blue containers, make great souvenirs.
Info: 11/r Borgo Albizi (at Viw Matteo Palmieri). Tel.
555/907315. No credit cards. www.vestri.it. Closed Sun.

Florence: Food Market
Mercato Centrale
The ground floor of the huge Central Market is loaded
with meat, fish and cheese. Upstairs you'll find fresh produce, wine, and homemade pasta. A great place to stock
up for a picnic! There's a modern food court upstairs with
plenty of places to eat. *Info*: Piazzale del Mercato Centrale
(between Via Nazionale and Via Sant' Antonino). Open
Mon-Fri 7am-2pm, Sat 7am-5pm, Closed Sun. Food Court
open daily 10am-midnight.

Genoa (Genova)
Le Cantine Squarciafico
Sit at long, shared tables in a medieval cellar and dine on
pesto-based dishes. The specialties here are *stoccafisso*
(dried cod) and *branzino alla ligure* (sea bass). Delicious
desserts. *Info*: 3R Piazza Invrea (near Piazza San
Lorenzo). Tel. 010/2470823. No lunch Sat. Closed most of
Aug. www.cantinesquarciafico.it. Moderate.

Retro
This comfortable, attractive restaurant is located in the
heart of Genoa, where you may be treated to live jazz
while dining. Excellent lobster *linguine*. You might want
to try the *orata al forno* (baked orata, a Mediterranean
fish *orata* which is similar to bream/gilthead). *Info*: 31
Via Malta (off of Via Brigata Liguria). Tel. 010/5535064.
Open daily. Moderate.

La Berlocca
Located in the heart of the historic center, this comfortable restaurant and wine bar will not disappoint. Genovese
dishes are the emphasis here. You can have a homemade
pasta dish like *tagliatelle al sugo di cinghiale* (tagliatelle

115

in a wild boar sauce) or *coniglio con olive e pinoli* (rabbit with olives and pine nuts). The house specialty here is *buridda* (salt cod with tomatoes and herbs). Good selection of Ligurian wines. *Info*: 45r Via dei Macelli di Soziglia. Tel. 010/7963333. Closed Mon. By eservation only on Sun. www.laberlocca.com. Moderate.

Focacceria Genovese
You can ask ten people from Genoa where to have the best *focaccia* and you'll likely get ten different answers. Genoa is known for this Ligurian specialty. In its simplest version, it's a flatbread topped with olive oil. Many are topped with cheese, olives, onions, and/or prosciutto. Great place for a quick snack while in the historic center. *Info*: 9r Piazza Fossatello. No phone. Inexpensive.

Genoa: Food Market
Mercato Orientale
This vibrant and colorful covered *mercato* (market) is a food lover's paradise. You'll find Italian cheese, fresh *focaccia* (flatbread with various toppings), meat, homemade pasta, fresh fish, fruits, and vegetables. Seek out the delicious Ligurian fig jam! *Info*: Main entrance on Via XX Settembre. Closed Sun.

Lucca
Giglio
A small *trattoria* known for seafood dishes. The homemade *tortelli* is delicious. Try the *tagliata di tonno* (grilled tuna). The outdoor patio is a lovely place to dine in good weather. The menu changes when the temperature cools, and you can sit inside by the fireplace and dine on such cold-weather dishes as *coniglio alla cacciatora con olive* (rabbit stew with olives). *Info*: 2 Piazza del Giglio. Tel. 0583/494058. Closed Tue, Wed (lunch) and part of Nov. www.ristorantegiglio.com. Moderate – Expensive.

Paris Boheme
You can dine on French and Italian dishes inside or outside (near the Puccini statue) at this friendly restaurant. Start with the *insalata erotica* (lettuce, fruit, and tomato salad), and try one of the excellent pasta dishes like *tortelli ai*

carciofi (tortelli pasta with artichokes). Very good house Chianti. *Info*: 6 Piazza Cittadella. Tel. 3389305275 (cell). Closed Tue. www.parisbohemelucca.com. Moderate.

Enoteca Calasto

Located on Piazza San Giovanni in Lucca's Old Town, this wine bar has both indoor and outdoor seating. There are over 150 labels of local wines (most from small producers). This really isn't a place for a meal, but they do serve salads, sandwiches, and pasta dishes (try the *tagliatelle* with *porcini* mushrooms). Wines by the glass start at €8. Wine tastings are offered, such as three wines from Lucca with a cheese-and-meat plate and coffee for €20. *Info*: 5 Piazza San Giovanni Tel. 058/3954267. www.lucca-wine-treasures.com. Inexpensive – Moderate.

Antica Bottega di Prospero

Lucca, and the area around it, is known for their olive oils. This food shop and deli sells olive oil and other regional specialties. Dried *porcini* mushrooms, dried fruit, and bottles of local wine can be purchased here and make great souvenirs. Info: 13 Via San Lucia. No phone.

Milan
Boeucc

Milan's oldest restaurant in an elegant setting near the Duomo. The *scalloppina con funghi porcini* (veal scallop in a porcini mushroom sauce) is fantastic. Known for its impeccabe service. *Info*: 2 Piazza Belgioioso. Tel. 02/76020224. Closed Sat, Sun (lunch) and Aug. Metro: Duomo. www. boeucc.it. Expensive.

Cavallini

Dine indoors or outside under the covered patio at this reasonably priced restaurant near the central train station. Try the *cotoletta alla milanese* (breaded veal cutlet) or *ravioli alla "Cavallini"* (homemade ravioli with meat sauce and cream). *Info*: 2 Via Mauro Macchi (at Via Napo Torriani). Tel. 02/6693174. Closed Sat (lunch) and Sun. Metro: Centrale. www.anticaosteriacavallini.it. Moderate.

Bar Martini/Martini Bistrot

Milan is synonymous with fashion. So it's not surprising that designers Dolce & Gabbana have opened this bar, lounge, and restaurant near one of their boutiques. Very trendy and very fashionable. More of a Milan design experience than a dining experience, although the food can be quite good – and the people-watching is excellent. *Info*: 15 Corso Venezia. Tel. 02/76011154. Open daily. Metro: San Babila. www.dolcegabbana.com/martini. Expensive.

Nerino Dieci

Great value at this attractive *trattoria* with a courteous staff. Try one of the many grilled dishes, including *pesce spada* (swordfish), *costolette di agnello* (lamb cutlet), or *gamberoni* (large prawns). *Info*: 10 Via Nerino (off of Via Torino). Tel. 02/39831019. Closed Sat (lunch) and Sun. Metro: Duomo. www.nerinodieci.it. Moderate.

Luini

You'll find this lunch-time favorite just one block from the cathedral and near the east entrance to the Galleria Vittorio Emanuele II. Here you'll find be the Milanese specialty *panzerotto*. Similar to a *calzone* or an *empanada*, the dough is slightly sweet and deep-fried, which gives them a crispy exterior. You can choose any number of ingredients, but most order the classic version with tomato sauce and mozzarella. This is food-on-the-go (there is nowhere to sit). A great idea if you're watching your euros, as they cost about €3. A popular choice is *cipolle, olive, e pomodoro* (onion, olives, and tomato). You can also order one baked like *mozzarella, pomodoro, acciughe, e olive nere* (mozzarella, tomato, anchovy, and black olives). There are also sweet versions, including *ricotta e rioccolato* (ricotta cheese and chocolate) and *castagne e mandorle* (chestnut and almond). *Info*: 16 Via Santa Radegonda. Tel. 02/86461917. Open Mon 10am-3pm, Tue-Sat 10am-8pm. Closed Sun. www.luini.it. Metro: Duomo. Inexpensive.

Al Pizzetta

This small, inexpensive, and comfortable *pizzeria* will not disappoint. Most of the small pizzas offered cost €3. Favorites include the *funghi* (mushroom), *salsic-*

cia (sausage), and *tonno e pomodori* (tuna and tomato sauce). Wash it down with a large glass of beer. *Info*: 73 Viale Monte Nero (near Piazza Cinque Giornate). Tel. 02/36508599. Closed Mon. No lunch Sat and Sun. Metro: Porta Romana. www.alpizzetta.it. Inexpensive.

La Latteria

There are only eight tables at this restaurant serving old-school northern Italian dishes. This blue-tiled spot was once a dairy shop selling eggs and milk. Over the years, they began serving such favorites as *risotto all Milanese*, *maccheroni al pomodoro e burro* (pasta with butter and tomatoes), and *bollito* (mixed meat stew). There are no reservations (and it's cash only), so you need to be there when the restaurant opens at 7:30pm. Locals fill the place up to sample chef and owner Arturo Maggi's dishes. An interesting experience. *Info*: 24 Via San Marco (off of via della Moscova). Tel. 02/6597653. Closed Sun. No reservations. No credit cards. Metro: Turati or Moscova. Moderate.

Il Salumaio di Montenapoleone

This is an interesting spot for lunch. There's a deli, cafe, and restaurant. The setting is the star attraction, as it's located in the neo-Renaissance courtyard of the Bagatti Valsecchi Museum. The neighborhood is filled with boutiques, so it's a good place to relax after shopping. Generous, homemade pasta dishes are the specialty here. Don't miss the *burrata*, a very buttery cheese from Apulia, the creamy *risotto milanese*, or the *pasta arrabbiata* (pasta with a spicy tomato and herb sauce). Interesting wine selection includes these two reds from Lombardy: *2007 Barbera Dodici Castello di Cigognola*, and *2009 Ferghettina Curtefranca 2009*. *Info*: 10 via S. Spirito/5 via Gesù. Tel 02/76001123. Closed Sun. Metro: Montenapoleone. www.ilsalumaiodimontenapoleone.it. Expensive. Metro: Montenapoleone.

Vertical

There's a warm welcome at this *enoteca* (wine bar) with modern décor. The walls are lined with shelves filled with bottles of wine. You'll chose from a list of wines by the glass or bottle from lesser-known wine producers. The limited menu features *antipasti*, a pizza of the day, and a veggie burger. Vertical is located in an area filled with other cafes, bars and restaurants. *Info*: At the corner of Viale Lazio and Viale Monte Nero. Tel. 392/1805287. Open 6:00pm - 1:00am. Open daily. www.verticalmilano.net. Metro: Porta Romana. Inexpensive-Moderate.

Milan: Pastry
Paticceria Marchesi

Marchesi has been serving pastries since 1824. Have a delicious cup of coffee with your treats. You must try the *cannoncini* (cream-filled puff pastry horns). *Info*: 11 via S. Maria alla Porta (off of via Meravigli). Tel. 02/862770. Open Mon-Sat 7:30am-8pm, Sun 8:30am-1pm. Closed Mon. www.pasticceriamarchesi.it. Metro: Cordusio.

Milan: Café
Caffè Miani (aka Zucca)

This café has been at the corner of the Piazza del Duomo and the Galleria Vittorio Emanuele II since 1867. It has a fantastic Belle Epoque interior, but the real attraction here is the great people-watching. You can order an *espresso* or sip an *aperitif* and watch the Milanese pass by. By the way, if you want to save some euros, drink at the bar. Prices increase if you are sitting at a table. *Info*: Galleria Vittorio Emanuele II. Tel. 02/86464435. Closed Mon and Aug. www.caffemiani.it. Metro: Duomo.

Milan: Food Stores
Peck

Founded in 1883, this temple to gourmet eating and drinking includes a bakery, prepared foods, deli, butcher shop, and renowned wine cellar. There's a tearoom upstairs that serves *salumi* and cheese platters, snacks, and drinks. *Info*: 9 Via Spadari. Tel.02/8023161. Shop closed Mon morning, Restaurant closed Mon. www.peck.it. Metro: Duomo.

Eataly Milano Smeraldo

Eataly is a chain of stores specializing in Italian food and wines. You'll find everything Italian, including pasta, beer, wine, meats, desserts, and vegetables. You can also eat and drink at one of the restaurants, bars, and cafes in this large space, and you can even take a cooking class! *Info*: 10 Piazza XXV Aprile. Tel. 02/49497301. Open daily 8:30am to midnight. www.eataly.net. Metro: Porta Garibaldi.

Brandi
Many places claim to have made the first pizza, but it's likely that the first *pizza margherita* (tomato, mozzarella, and basil) was made here. They also serve pasta dishes. So what if it's touristy? *Info*: 2 Salita Santa Anna di Palazzo (off of Via Chiaia). Tel. 081/416928. Open daily. www. brandipizzeria.com. Inexpensive – Moderate.

Gino Sorbillo
You'll most likely have to wait outside before you get to order your delicious pizza at this crowded and lively *pizzeria*. The pizzas are large, and you'll have a long list to choose from. The specialties here are the simple *pizza marinara* (tomatoes and oregano) or the hearty *pizza quattro stagione* (cheese, proscuitto, salami, cheese, and mushroom). Be careful, as there are other eateries on the street that use "Sorbillo" in their name (pizza places set up by other family members). *Info*: 32 Via dei Tribunali. Tel. 081/446643. Closed Sun and part of Aug. www.sorbillo.it. Inexpensive.

Da Michele
Just as crowded as Sorbillo above, this *pizzeria* (open since 1870) was featured in the Julia Roberts film "Eat, Pray, Love." You'll need to get a number and likely wait for a while. There are only two offerings here: *pizza marinara* (tomato, oregano, and garlic) and *pizza margherita* (tomato, mozzarella, and basil). *Info*: 1 Via Sersale (off of Corso Umberto between Piazza N. Amore and Piazza Garibaldi). Tel. 081/5539204. No credit cards. Closed Sun and part of Aug. www.damichele.net. Inexpensive.

Antico Forno delle Sfogliatelle Calde Fratelli Attanasio
Just a few blocks from the central train station, this old bakery is the place to have *sfogliatelle*, meaning many leaves or layers. These crisp, layered pastries resemble

seashells when baked, and are filled with sweetened *ricotta*, semolina, cinnamon, and candied orange or lemon zest. When you arrive, take a number first and then get ready to taste this delicious traditional Neapolitan pastry. *Info*: 1-4 Vico Ferrovia . Tel. 081/285675. Open 6:30am to 7:30pm. Closed Mon. www.sfogliatelleattanasio.it. Inexpensive.

L'Ebbrezza di Noe

This is an *enoteca* (wine bar) during the day and a restaurant for dinner. You'll sit in small rooms surrounded by bottles of wine on shelves. The owner Luca and his staff are friendly and attentive, and will guide you through ordering one of the many wines from the Campania region that are available here. The menu changes frequently (there's no written menu, only a blackboard menu). The *antipasti* features a mixture of six meats, cheeses, a quail egg, toast, and eggplant. The specialty here is *carpaccio di chianina* (thinly sliced raw Tuscan steak). A real find and an excellent place to experience wine from small local producers. *Info*: 8-9 Vicolo Vetriera a Chiaia. Tel. 081/400104. Closed Mon and Sun (dinner). www.lebbrezzadinoe.com. Moderate.

Tandem

This homey, no-frills *trattoria* specializes in *ragu*. There are two choices: vegetarian and meat. You can choose pasta as a base, or just dip thick pieces of bread into the sauce. The menu also features staples such as meatballs and pork dishes, but most come here for the *ragu*. You can purchase the house wines (including a surprisingly good sparkling *rosso*) by the carafe or glass. *Info*: 51 Via G. Paladino (off of Piazzetta Nilo). Tel: 081/19002468. Open daily. www.ristorantetandemragu.it. Inexpensive.

Palazzo Petrucci

This elegant restaurant with minimalist décor, located in a villa overlooking the Gulf of Naples, serves innovative dishes. For your starter try the delicious *zuppa di castagne* (chestnut soup) that includes beans and *pancetta* (cured pork belly). Main courses include *agnello con albicocche, pecorino e menta* (lamb served with apricots, pecorino cheese, and mint). They also have a five-course tasting menu for €60. You'll be given a complimentary glass of *prosecco* when you arrive, and the restaurant has an extensive wine list. *Info*: 16/c Via Posillipo (new location as of 2016). Tel. 081/5757538. Closed Sun (dinner), Mon (lunch), and part of Aug. www.palazzopetrucci.it. Expensive.

La Stanza del Gusto
This restaurant is known for its mixture of traditional Neapolitan cuisine and international fare. It has one of the best wine lists in the city, and is also known for excellent pastry. You can dine in two spots. Squistezze is the casual (and less expensive) ground-floor cheese bar serving salads, soups, burgers, and (of course) a large selection of Italian cheeses. The menu in the upstairs restaurant changes almost daily, and can include *zuppa di lenticchie* (lentil soup) and *stinco di maiale* (braised pork shank). *Info*: 100 Via Costantinopoli. Tel. 081/401578. Closed Sun, Mon (lunch), and part of Aug. Reservations required at restaurant.
www.lastanzadelgusto.com. Moderate – Expensive

Trattoria del Golfo
If you're looking for a friendly, moderately priced *trattoria* in Naples, this will fit the bill. Try the seafood *antipasti* featuring a mix of seafood including shrimp and calamari. For a main course, order the *spaghetti alla vongole* (spaghetti with clams). Portions are large and satisfying. Good regional wine and grappa selection. *Info*: 56 Via Santa Brigida (off of Via Verid). Tel. 081/19247380. Open daily. Moderate.

Orvieto
Le Grotte del Funaro
Umbrian specialties served in a *grotte* (cave). Windows provide a sweeping view of the countryside below. Try the *ravioli con brasato di chianina* (ravioli with braised beef). The specialty here is *grigliata mista* (a plate of grilled meats including sausage, lamb, and pork). *Info*: 41 Via Ripa Serancia. Tel. 0763/343276. Closed Mon and part of Jul. www.grottedelfunaro.it. Moderate.

Osteria Numero Uno
This warm and friendly restaurant (with whimsical décor) in the historic center of town will not disappoint. Start with

123

the tasty *flan di spinaci con crema di gorgonzola* (spinach flan with gorgonzola cream), and try one of the delicious pasta dishes like *strozzapreti con zucchine, melanzane e peperoni* (strozzapreti pasta with zucchini, eggplant, and peppers). *Info*: 2/A Via Ripa Corsica (at the corner of Via della Pace). Tel. 0763/341845. Closed Mon. www.osterianumerouno.eu. Moderate.

Enoteca Al Duomo

This *enoteca* (wine bar) and wine shop is located on Piazza Duomo. You can sip your wine while you view the façade of the town's fantastic Gothic cathedral. In addition to cheese and meat plates, you can order pasta dishes and *panini* (sandwiches). This is the place in Orvieto to have a glass of *Orvieto Classico*, the delicious local wine made from Trebbiano grapes. *Info*: 13 Piazza Duomo. Tel. 076/3344607. www.enotecaduomo.com. Inexpensive – Moderate.

Padua

Padua is known for its outdoor-café culture. When the sun starts to set, head to one of the large squares in the city (**Piazza delle Frutta** or **Piazza delle Erbe**) and order an *aperitif*. *Campari* (a red liqueur with a bitter taste) is popular here, especially as a *spritz* (a mixture of Campari, wine, and soda water).

Belle Parti

Innovative versions of regional dishes served at this attractive restaurant located in the center of Padua (a few blocks from Piazza dei Signori). This is the place to splurge in Padua. It's known for it fish dishes. The specialty here is the interesting *zuppetta di pesce con peperoncino fresco* (fish soup with *peperoncini*). Always a warm welcome. *Info*: 11 via Belle Parti. Tel. 049/8751822. Closed Sun. www.ristorantebelleparti.it. Expensive.

Enotavola

Pino, the owner, clearly loves his wine bar and restaurant with simple, modern décor. For an appetizer, order the interesting *tartare di tonno allo zenzero con riso venere* (tuna tartare with ginger and black rice). For a pasta dish, try the *gnocchi su salsa di baccalà, con croccante di pinoli alle erbe aromatiche* (potato gnocchi in a cod sauce with pine nuts and aromatic herbs).

The decent wine list features wine from throughout Italy (with a few from France). *Info*: 37 Via dell'Arco (at Via Marsala). Tel. 049/8762385. Closed Mon, Sun (lunch), and most of Aug. www.enotavola.com. Moderate.

Enoteca dei Tadi

The dining room in this friendly *enoteca* (wine bar) and restaurant seats about only 20, so you should try to make reservations. Start your dinner with the fresh *insalata Tadi*, a salad with tomatoes, cucumbers, olives, and *sfilacci di cavallo* (a local specialty of shredded dried horse meat). You can order four different kinds of *lasagna*, and several dishes featuring *baccalà* (salt cod). A good selection of wines from the Veneto region by the glass and bottle. *Info*: 16 Via dei Tadi, Tel. 338/4083434. Closed Mon. No lunch. www.enotecadeitadi.it. Moderate.

Osteria dei Fabbri

If you're visiting from Venice, you'll find the price of wining and dining is significantly cheaper in Padua. This casual, inexpensive eatery is located near the busy Piazza del Erbe. Service is friendly, and you can order *ossobuco* (braised veal shank) or one of many pasta dishes, like *orecchiette con gamberi e broccoli* (ear-shaped pasta with shrimp and broccoli). *Info* : 13 Via dei Fabbri. Tel. 049/6503366. Closed Sun. Inexpensive – Moderate.

Caffè Pedrocchi

No visit to Padua would really be complete without a visit to this huge, elegant, and historic coffeehouse. *Info*: 15 Piazzetta Pedrocchi/15 Via VIII Febbraio (off of Piazza Cavour). Tel. 049/8781231. Closed Mon. www.caffepedrocchi.it.

Palermo
Antica Focacceria San Francesco

Stuffed focaccia sandwiches and Sicilian snacks at this 1834 bakery in the heart of Old Town. Delicious *arancini* (deep-fried rice balls). A Palermo institution. *Info*: 58 Via Paternostro. Tel. 091/320264. Open daily. www.anticafocacceria.it. Inexpensive.

Ottava Nota
Innovative Sicilian dishes are served at this modern restaurant
in the Kalsa district. Start with the *tartare di tonno e avocado*
(tuna tartar and avocado). Other dishes include the tasty *risotto
con asparagi e gambero* (risotto with asparagus and shrimp)
and *petto d'anatra all'arancia* (duck breast with orange).
Attentive service and a wine list featuring lesser-known Sicilian
wines. *Info*: 55 Via Butera. Tel. 091/6168601. Closed Sun
and Mon (lunch). www.ristoranteottavanota.it. Moderate –
Expensive.

Ristorante Cin Cin
Traditional Sicilian dishes are updated at this attractive restaurant near Via Liberta (a main shopping street in Palermo). For
a starter, order the *insalata di gamberetti e frutta, con salsetta
di yogurt e papavero* (shrimp and fruit salad with yogurt and
poppy-seed dressing). Pasta dishes include *gnocchi freschi con
gorgonzola e rucola* (fresh *gnocchi* with *gorgonzola* cheese
and arugula). For your main course (if you still have room) try
filetto di vitello al Marsala con radicchio e noci (beef filet with
Marsala wine, radicchio and walnuts). The dessert specialty is
semifreddo (a fluffy, sliceable ice cream) which is served here
in a Marsala- and-raisin sauce. The excellent wine list features
Sicilian labels with an emphasis on small producers.
Info: 22 Via Manin. Tel. 091/6124095. Closed Sun. No lunch.
www.ristorantecincin.com. Moderate.

Casa del Brodo
This restaurant near the Vucciria Market (see below) has
been in business since the late 1800s. If you're interested in
no-nonsense Sicilian dishes, come here to try *macco di fave*
(meatballs and tripe) or *fritella di fave* (fried fava beans). The
house specialty is the hearty *tortellini in brodo* (homemade
pasta in a beef broth). *Info*: 175 Corso Vittorio Emanuele. Tel.
091/321655. Closed Tue and Sun from Jun to Sep. www.casa-
delbrodo.it. Inexpensive – Moderate.

Antico Caffè Spinnato
Dating back to 1860, this is Palermo's oldest café. Sicilians
are known for their sweets, and you can sample scrumptious
cakes, cocktails, coffee and *gelati* here. *Info*: 115 Via Principe
di Belmonte. Tel. 091/583231. www.spinnato.it.

Vucciria Market

In the heart of the *centro storico*, this market is filled with colorful vendors, fresh produce, stinky cheese, and hanging meats. It's really worth the trip to experience the sights and smells. Not to be missed are the stands selling olives, artichokes, and flavorful blood oranges. Info: The streets around the Piazza San Domenico. Open dawn to 2pm. Closed Sun.

Ballarò Market

It's said that a food market has been on this site for 1000 years. You'll find vendors selling vegetables, cheeses, spices, meat, and fresh fish. There are plenty of stands for you to have a snack. Seek out the stands selling *panelle* (slices of dough made from chickpeas that are deep-fried with slices of eggplant). Also popular here is the Palermo specialty of *pane ca' meusa* (calf's-spleen topped with cheese). *Info*: The streets around Piazza Carmine (between Via Marqueda and Corso Tukory). In the Albergheria district. Open dawn to 2pm.

Palermo: Cooking Class

Ristorante Cin Cin offers cooking classes which include a visit to a local food market. Reservations can be made through their website at www.ristorantecincin.com and cost €150 per person.

Perugia
La Taverna

Traditional Umbrian food (great lamb) and attentive service in a medieval house in the heart of the historic center. Try the *filetto di tonno fresco in crosta di pepe* (tuna filet cooked in a pepper crust). The restaurant is known for its grilled foods. Try the *grigliata di carne miste* (mixed grilled meats) or *grigliata di verdure con pecorino* (grilled vegetables with pecorino cheese). The chef Claudio oversees everything. *Info*: 8 Via delle Streghe (off Corso Vannucci). Tel. 075/5724128. Open daily. www.ristorantelataverna.com. Moderate.

Bottega del Vino

Perugia is a lively city as it is home to a large university population. This wine bar/restaurant is always busy. Located off of the Piazza November IV (one of the city's main squares), you can sample wines by the glass and watch the world go by. Umbrian cheeses and meats are served here, along with pasta and salads. Perugia hosts Umbria Jazz, a huge jazz festival each July. You can listen to live jazz here on many evenings until closing at midnight. *Info*: 1 Via del Sole. Tel. 075/5716181. Closed Jan. No lunch Sun and Mon. Moderate.

Perugina
Perugia hosts the popular Eurochocolate Festival every October. If you love chocolate, you'll think that you died and went to heaven at this chocolate shop that has been in business since 1907. Try *baci*, bite-sized chocolates with a whole hazelnut in the center. If the shop isn't open, you can buy the chocolates at shops throughout the city. *Info*: 101 Corso Vannucci. Tel. 075/5736677. Open daily. You can tour the chocolate factory *Casa del Cioccolato* outside of Perugia. Information and booking at www.perugina.com.

Pisa
Il Bistrot
This friendly, intimate restaurant and wine bar is located between the train station and the Leaning Tower. Start with the delicious *bruschetta*. For your first course, order *pasta Pic*i (pasta with cheese, pears, and black pepper) and try the *filetto di maialino* (pork tenderloin) in a gorgonzola sauce. Order a bottle of *Degli Azzoni Avogadro Carradori Helianthus* (a blend of Sangiovese, Merlot, and Syrah) from a local vineyard. A real find. *Info*: 17 Piazza Chiara Gambacorti. Tel. 349/0759809. Closed Wed. No lunch Sat and Sun from July to Sep. www.ilovebistrot.it. Moderate.

La Sosta dei Cavalieri
This intimate and friendly restaurant is a great choice for lunch or dinner. It's a short walk from the Leaning Tower. Try the delicious *tagliolini al sugo di piccione* (thin noodles with a pigeon sauce) or the *cannelloni alla erbe di campo e pinoli* (cannelloni with wild herbs and pine nuts). *Info*: 3 Via San Frediano (off of Piazza dei Cavalieri). Tel. 050/9912410. Closed Sun and part of Aug. www.sostadeicavalieri.it. Moderate.

Osteria die Cavalieri

Not to be confused with the nearby La Sosta dei Cavalieri, this restaurant with stone walls is a favorite in Pisa. There are two seatings for dinner (7:30pm and 9:00pm). For you first course, order the *tagliatelline al coniglio e asparagi* (tagliatelline pasta with rabbit and asparagus). This is a good choice for vegetarian, dining as most dishes also have a vegetarian option like the *tagliatelline ai funghi* (tagliatelline pasta in a mushroom sauce). The main course of *filetto di manzo alla griglia* (grilled beef tenderloin) is delicious. There are also daily fresh fish specials. *Info*: 16bVia San Frediano (off of Piazza dei Cavalieri). Tel. 050/580858. Closed Sun. www.osteriacavalieri.pisa.it. Moderate.

Vicolo Divino

This attractive wine bar with a stone floor and outdoor seating in warm weather is located near the River Arno. The staff is welcoming, and the local wine selection is excellent. You'll be offered (free) snacks from the small buffet at the bar, or you can order a cheese-and-meat platter. *Info*: 10 Filippo Serafini (off of Lungarno Pacinotti). Tel. 377/9428446. Closed Sun. No lunch Thu and Sat. www.vicolodivino.it. Inexpensive – Moderate.

Portofino

Puny

Portofino may just be the most picturesque port town in Italy. Dining here is not cheap. This restaurant has a great location on the *piazza* at the harbor. Great people-watching while you dine on Ligurian specialties like *pappardelle al portofino* (pappardelle pasta in a tomato and pesto sauce). Fresh seafood dishes, especially those with *gamberi* (shrimp), are featured on the menu. *Info*: 5 Piazza Martiri dell'Olivetta. Tel. 0185/269037. Closed Thu, Jan, and Feb. Expensive – Very Expensive.

Il Pitosforo

Famous and very expensive, this harborside restaurant serves Ligurian specialties. Known for its *zuppa di pesce* (fish stew). You can't beat the view. *Info*: 8-9 Via Molo Umberto I. Tel. 0185/269020. Closed Mon, Tue, and Dec to Feb. www.pitosforo-portofino.it. Expensive – Very Expensive.

Winterose

There are only a few tables at this wine bar and wine shop. Prices start at €12 for a glass of local wine. While that may seem expensive, you're in one of the priciest places in Italy. Your glass of wine comes with an *antpasti* plate with cheeses, olives, chips, and meats. Located on the water, this is a wonderful place for people-watching, and the view is spectacular. Service is warm and friendly. *Info*: 42 Calata Marconi. No phone. www.wineroseportofino.it. Usually open in high season from 10am to 8pm. Moderate.

Ravenna

Bella Venezia

If you're visiting for the day, this is a good choice for an elegant lunch, as it's located near the Piazza del Popolo (the town's main square). Enjoy regional dishes, especially *cappelletti alla romagnola* (cap-shaped pasta stuffed with ricotta cheese, chicken and/or pork, and nutmeg). Its other specialty is *cotoletta alla Bisanzio* (fried veal cutlet topped with cherry tomatoes). *Info*: 16 Via Novembre IV (Centro Storico). Tel. 0544/212746. Closed Sun. www.ristorantebellavenezia.it. Moderate – Expensive.

Cinema Alexander

This interesting restaurant is located in a former movie theater. The attractive building dates back to the 1800s. You'll dine on local specialties surrounded by film posters. There are two tasting menus (one featuring meat and the other seafood). Try the *tonno* (tuna) or the *piccione* (pigeon). *Info*: 8 Via Bassa del Pignataro. Tel. 0544/212967. Closed Mon and Sun (in summer). www.ristorantealexander.it. Moderate – Expensive.

Cupido Piadina d'Oro

Nothing fancy at this tiny restaurant located near Piazza Andrea Costa (near the Piazza del Popolo). You can order simple homemade pasta dishes, lasagna, pizza, and *piadina* (a soft flatbread). Try it stuffed with *proscuitto* and cheese, or order their gluten-free *piadina*. *Info*: 43/A Via Camillo Benso Cavour. Tel. 0544/37529. Open daily. www.piadacupido.net. Inexpensive – Moderate.

Gastronomia Marchesini

This food shop and deli specializes in regional products. There's also a restaurant on the premises, and for a cheaper option, a self-service eatery with a large buffet. *Info*: 2 Via Mazzini. Tel. 0544/212309. www.ristorantimarchesini.com.

Food Market

Ravenna's colorful **Mercato Coperto** (Covered Market) is located near the center of town on Piazza Andrea Costa, and has been at this location since 1869. The market, filled with produce, fish, meat, flowers, and household items, is presently closed for renovations but is slated to reopen in 2017.

Rome   *See Rome maps pages 154-158*

L'Angolo Divino

Taste and buy wines from every region of Italy at this pleasant wine bar near the Camp de'Fiori. Have a light lunch or dinner, as they serve salads, cured meats, and cheese. *Info*: 12 Via dei Balestrari (near the Campo de' Fiori). Tel. 06/6864413. Closed Mon (lunch), Sun (lunch), and part of Aug. www.angolodivino.it Inexpensive – Moderate. Map C, #1.

Antica Roma

This unique *hostaria* is built into ancient ruins about three miles outside central Rome (about a 20-minute taxi ride). Always a warm welcome. You'll dine on Roman and Mediterranean specialties. Try the *mazzancolle al vino blanc* (large prawns in a white-wine sauce), *salmone con le mandorle* (salmon in an almond-and-cream sauce), or *scaloppini al marsala* (thin slices of veal in a Marsala-wine sauce). An experience. *Info*: 87 Via Appia Antica. Tel. 06/5132888. Closed Mon. www.anticaroma.it. Moderate – Expensive.

Antico Arco

Attentive service, a modern setting, and fine Roman food make this a popular place. Excellent *carrè di agnello* (rack of lamb). Delicious chocolate desserts. It's a little out of the way at the top of Janiculum Hill. The wine list has 1200 selections from Italy and all over the world. You can order a bottle of the house *Chianti* for €18 or *La Tache Romanée Conti 2009* for €1,800 (we opted for the *Chianti*). *Info*: 7 Piazzale Aurelio. Tel. 06/5815274. Open daily. www.anticoarco.it. Moderate – Expensive. Map C, #2.

Antico Caffé della Pace

Attractive cafe with indoor and outdoor seating. Great place for a relaxing drink and snack near the Church of Santa Maria della Pace. *Info*: 3 Via della Pace (near Piazza Navona). Tel. 06/6861216. Open daily. www.caffedellapace.it. Inexpensive. Map B, #3.

Babette

Inspired by the film "Babette's Feast," your feast should include the *filetto di manzo alla griglia* (grilled beef filet served with a basil sauce). Great buffet lunch. The wine list features over 100 selections from Italy and France. Opt for the *Casale del Giglio Chardonnay* from Lazio (the area around Rome). There's a charming courtyard where you can dine in summer. *Info*: 1D-3 Via Margutta. Tel. 06/3211559. Closed Mon and part of Jan. www.babetteristorante.it. Moderate – Expensive. Map A, #4.

Il Bacaro

Small, unpretentious restaurant on a small alley near the Piazza delle Copelle (a huge ivy covers the entrance). You are welcomed with a complimentary glass of *prosecco* and a small appetizer. Delicious *risotto* dishes, and try the *involtini di pesce spada con gamberi* (swordfish roulades with shrimp) or *ventaglio di tonno con pomodori secchi e riduzione di aceto balsamico* (tuna with sun-dried tomatoes and balsamic vinegar). *Info*: 27 Via degli Spagnoli. Tel. 06/6872554. Closed Tue. No lunch Mon-Fri from Nov-Feb. www.ilbacaroroma.com. Moderate-Expensive. Map B, #5.

Osteria del Cavaliere

This small, unpretentious, family-owned restaurant serves Italian fare with an emphasis on dishes from the Abruzzo region. You'll receive a warm welcome and dine with mostly locals. Try the *chicche di patate ai 5 formaggi* (small potato gnocchi with five cheeses) or the *tagliata di manzo alla griglia* (sliced grilled beef). Don't be put off by its somewhat out-of-the-way location. *Info*: 32 Via Alba (between Via Appia Nuova and Via Tuscolana). Tel. 06/64850434. Closed Sun. No lunch. www.osteriadelcavaliere.com. Moderate.

Centro

It's often difficult to find good places to eat near a main train station. This new restaurant (which opened in the fall of 2016) is near the Termini train station and is an exception to that rule. The hamburger "Centro" is a popular choice. It's served with cheddar cheese and a barbeque sauce. For more Italian fare, try the *spaghetti cacio e pepe* (*spaghetti* served with a sauce made of black pepper and *pecorino* cheese). The rich *fondant al cioccolato* is served with an orange sauce. Very friendly service. *Info*: 61 Via Cavour. Tel. 06/48913935. Open daily for breakfast, lunch, and dinner. www.centrorestaurant.it. Moderate. Map D, #13.

Cavour 313

A huge wine list and selection of cured meats and cheeses make this a good place for a light meal. The pork tenderloin crusted with pistachio nuts is delicious. *Info*: 313 Via Cavour (near the Forum and Colosseum). Tel. 06/6785496. Closed part of Aug. www.cavour313.it. Inexpensive – Moderate. Map D, #7.

Cul de Sac

Wines from throughout the world are offered at this wine bar near Piazza Navona. Nice selection of wines by the glass. A plus is the outdoor seating that stays open until a bit past midnight. The interesting menu features everything from duck ravioli to roast beef in an "esterhazy" sauce (with mushrooms, sour cream, and paprika). You can also order salads and sweets here. Great people-watching. The wine list here resembles a telephone book, and features over 1500 selections. *Info*: 73 Piazza Pasquino. Tel. 06/68801094. Open daily. www.enotecaculdesacroma.it. Map B, #8.

Dar Poeta

Choose thick- or thin-crust pizza at this popular and inexpensive eatery in the Trastevere neighborhood. If you have room, try the *calzone* with Nutella (chocolate-hazelnut spread) and *ricotta* cheese. *Info*: 45 Vicolo del Bologna (off of Via della Scala). Tel. 06/5880516. Open daily. www.darpoeta.com. Inexpensive – Moderate. Map C, #9.

Enoteca Corsi
Wine bar serving Roman cuisine at common-seating tables in a 1937 storefront. An economical choice for lunch. Try the white lasagna with artichokes. Be advised that this restaurant is in many guidebooks and can often be filled with tourists. *Info*: 87/88 Via del Gesú (off of Via del Plebescito). Tel. 06/6790821. Closed Sun and Aug. Lunch only. www.enotecacorsi.com. Inexpensive. Map B, #10.

'Gusto
You'll find something for every food lover at this complex located on and around the Piazza Augusto Imperatore.

A *ristorante* (restaurant), *pizzeria*, and cookware shop are at #9 on the piazza.

The wine bar at 23 Via della Frezza serves wines from through-out Italy.

There's a comfortable *caffé* at #28 serving excellent Italian coffee and desserts.

Our favorite is **'Gusto Osteria**, at 16 Via della Frezza. The *osteria* serves hearty traditional Roman fare. Try the delicious *pasta cacio e pepe* (pasta with pecorino, parmesan cheese and black pepper). There's a glass-enclosed *formaggeria* (cheese shop) tucked into the corner of the *osteria* featuring cheeses from throughout Italy.

Info: 9 Piazza Augusto Imperatore (near Via del Corso). Tel. 06/3226273 (restaurant, cookware shop, *pizzeria*, and wine bar). Tel. 06/3236363 (Shop). Tel. 06/32111482 (*osteria* and cheese shop). Tel 06/68134221 (*caffé*). Open daily. www.gusto.it. Inexpensive – Expensive. Map A, #11.

Il Convivio
Elegant and acclaimed restaurant. It's formal with what can be described as old-fashioned décor. The food is excellent, but whatever you have, make sure you start your dinner with the memorable *fiori di zucca in pastella con mozzarella* (fried zucchini flowers filled with mozzarella cheese). *Info*: 28 Vicolo dei Soldati (between Piazza Navona and Piazza Umberto I). Tel.

06/6869432. Closed Sun and part of Aug. No lunch.
www.ilconviviotroiani.com. Expensive – Very Expensive.
Map B, #12.

Polese

Enjoy outdoor and indoor dining at this *trattoria* on the charming Piazza Sforza Cesarini. Try the *fettuccine alla Polese*
(fettuccine w/cream and mushrooms). *Info*: 40 Piazza Sforza
Cesarini (off of Corso Vittorio Emanuele not too far from
Piazza Navona). Tel. 06/6861709. Closed Tue. www.tratto-
riapolese.com. Moderate. Map B, #14.

Another *trattoria* on the same piazza at #24 is **Da Luigi.** Try
the delicious *penne alla vodka.* Tel. 06/6865946. Closed Mon.
www.trattoriadaluigi.com. Moderate. Map B, #14.

La Terrazza dell'Eden

This very expensive and formal restaurant (jacket and tie
required) in the Hotel Eden (several blocks off the Via Veneto)
offers memorable food and an unforgettable view of St. Peter's.
It's known for its veal tartare starter and its braised *Chianina*
beef. *Info*: 49 Via Ludovisi. Tel. 06/478121. Open daily.
www.laterrazzadelleden.com. Very Expensive. Map A, #15.

Vini e Buffet

This unpretentious Roman eatery with friendly staff is off the
Campo Marzio and Via del Corso. The entrance to the small
restaurant is covered with vines. You'll sit at wooden tables
where you can order sandwiches, vegetarian dishes, salads,
soups, or pasta. At lunch, workers from the nearby Parliament
drop in, and in the evening the place is quieter and less
crowded. There's also a decent selection of wine by the glass or
bottle. *Info*: 60 Vicolo della Torretta. Tel. 06/6871445. Closed
Sun. Inexpensive – Moderate. Map A, #16.

Vinoteca Novecento

This small wine bar has a good selection of wine, *prosecco*,
and *grappa*. This is a great place to have a cheese-and-salami
plate or a plate of meatballs while trying wine from all regions
of Italy. You can sit outside on tables made of wine barrels in
good weather, or inside surrounded by walls decorated with
wine crates and jammed with wine bottles. *Info*: 47 Piazza

Delle Coppelle (near Piazza Navona). Tel. 06/6833078. Open daily. Moderate. Map A, #17.

Enoteca Ferrara

This interesting place in the Trastevere neighborhood provides plenty of options for wining and dining. Housed in a building dating back to the 1400s, you can see the large wine cellar through an ancient grate. We like to enjoy a glass of wine and appetizers at "La Mescita," the wine bar. If you want to dine, you have two options: Ferrarino's Tavern is an *osteria* where you can have the house *gnocchi* served with either clams or Spanish ham. The more formal and expensive namesake restaurant serves innovative dishes featuring everything from guinea fowl (*faraona*) to *baccalà* (cod). *Info*: 41 Piazza Trilussa. Tel. 06/58333920. Open daily for dinner. Lunch Sunday only. Closed Sundays in August. www.enotecaferrara.it. Moderate (*osteria*) – Expensive (restaurant). Map C, #18.

Rome: Food and Wine Stores

Eataly

Roam through 170,000 square feet crammed with Italian food and specialties. There are 18 restaurants and cafes, a brewery, coffee shops, and food and wine shops. A must for every foodie. *Info*: 1492 Via 12 Ottobre (in the Air Terminal next to Stazione Ostiense). Piramide metro. Take the underpass to Stazione Ostiense. Five-minute walk to the Air Terminal. Tel. 06/90279201. Open daily 10am to midnight (individual shops and restaurants have different hours of operation). www.roma.eataly.it.

Buccone

This wine bar is a great place for lunch, and you can also buy wines from every region of Italy. *Info*: 19 Via di Ripetta (near the Piazza del Popolo). Tel. 06/3612154. Lunch Mon-Sat. Dinner Fri-Sat. Closed Sun. www.enotecabuccone.com.

Castroni

A food market offering specialties from every region of Italy. Huge pasta selection. *Info*: 196 Via Cola di Rienzo (near San Pietro). Tel. 06/6874383. Open daily. www.castronicoladirienzo.it.

Moriondo e Gariglio

Many of the 80 delicacies that are for sale at this historic chocolate shop (established in 1850) are made with the same 19th-century recipes. Don't miss the dark-chocolate truffles! *Info*: 21 Via Piè di Marmo. Tel. 06/6990856. Closed Sun.

Palatium: Enoteca Regionale del Lazio

Wine bar, restaurant and shop selling regional culinary products and wine. Delicious *antipasti*, especially the *carciofi alla romana* (artichokes stuffed with garlic, parsley and mint, cooked in olive oil and white wine). They also sponsor wine tastings featuring the wines of the Lazio region. *Info*: 94 Via Frattina (near the Spanish Steps). Tel. 06/69202132. Closed Sun.

Trimani

180-year-old store with over 5,000 wines, liqueurs and *grappas*. *Info*: 20 Via Goito (near Stazione Termini). Tel. 06/4469661. Closed Sat-Sun. www.trimani.com.

The **Trimani Wine Bar** is around the corner at 37/b Via Cernaia (Closed Sun).

Rome: Coffee
Tazza d'Oro

This coffee shop near the Pantheon is a great place to taste great Italian coffee (*caffè*). On a hot day in Rome, try a *granita de caffè* (coffee served over crushed ice) and on a chilly day, get a thick, rich, and decadent hot chocolate (*cioccolata calda*). Go to the cash register to order and then take your receipt to the counter. *Info*: 84 Via degli Orfani. Tel. 06/6789792. Open daily. www.tazzadorocoffeeshop.com.

Rome: Gelato
Giolitti

Everyone seems to have an opinion on the best place to have *gelato*. So, head to this shop near the Pantheon like others have for over a century. It's especially known for its variety of fruit flavors. *Info*: 40 Via degli Uffici del Vicario (next to the Camera dei Deputati della Repubblica Italiana). Tel. 06/6991243. Open daily 7am to 1:30am. www.giolitti.it.

Gelateria dei Gracchi

Get in line for some of the best *gelato* in all of Italy. This shop, a short walk from the Vatican, uses all-natural ingredients. Known for its delicious pistachio. We loved the dark chocolate! *Info*: 272 Via dei Gracchi. Tel. 06/6876606. Open daily.

Gelateria Vice

Part of a chain, this *gelateria* is known for its ice cream made from organic ingredients. The Amalfi lemon is delicious. *Info*: 9 Corso Vittorio Emanuele. Tel. 06/88930218. www.viceitalia.it.

Rome: Food Markets
Campo de' Fiori

at Via del Giubbonari
7am-1:30pm, Mon-Sat.
A food market has been held here since the 1800s. Even if you're not food shopping, head to this attractive square to get a glimpse of Roman life.

Nuovo Mercato di Testaccio

Via Benjamin Franklin (between Via Luigi Galvani and Via Aldo Manuzio)
7am-2pm, Mon-Sat.
The Testaccio Market has moved to a new, modern building. Filled with colorful vendors, stinky cheese, fresh produce, poultry, and meat. www.mercatotestaccio.com.

Nuovo Mercato Trionfale

at Via Andrea Doria (near the Cipro Metro stop)
7am-2pm, Mon-Sat. Open until 5pm on Tue and Fri.
There are 250 vendors at this crowded and popular food market.

Rome: Cooking Classes

The restaurant **Enoteca Corsi** (above) sponsors cooking classes held in a medieval castle in Rome. Your host, Dario, is an expert on Italian art. He'll guide you around the castle and discuss its works of art. Claudia Paiella is a *sommelier* who will walk you through the process of shopping at Rome's food markets for the fresh ingredients used in traditional Roman dishes. Classes and lunch are held in the apartments of Pope Paolo

V and Pope Leo XII. This one-day class is a unique cooking-and-art seminar. *Info*: Reservations can be made through the Enoteca Corsi website www.enotecacorsi.com or through www.3inchfat.com. There are several other tours and classes available. Prices start at €180.

Bel Soggiorno

Tuscan specialties served in a 100-year-old hotel located in this beautiful walled town. For your first course, have the *pappardelle di pasta fresca al sugo di cinghiale* (fresh pappardelle pasta in wild-boar sauce). For a main course, the *costolette d'agnello* (lamp chop) is delicious. Lots of game dishes on the menu. Fantastic views of the countryside from the terrace. *Info*: 91 Via San Giovanni (in the Hotel Bel Soggiorno). Tel. 0577/943149. Closed Wed, part of Nov, Dec, part of Feb, and part of Mar. www.ristorante-belsoggiorno.it. Moderate – Expensive.

Enoteca di Vinorum

San Gimignano is crowded with day trippers, so if you want or need a break from the crowds (especially in high season), this wine bar is a good choice. Housed in former stables, if you score a table outside (there are only six tables) you'll be rewarded with a scenic view. Good selection of *antipasti* (cheese, meats, bruschetta, salads) and an excellent selection of wine by the glass. This is the place to try *Vernaccia di San Gimignano*, a local dry white wine with a slight peppery taste. *Info*: 30 Piazza della Cisterna/5 Via degli Innocenti. Tel. 0577/907192. open daily. Moderate.

Dorandò

This small and elegant restaurant is housed in a 14th-century building in the center of town. You'll dine on Tuscan specialties such as *controfiletto al Chianti Classico* (sirloin in a Chianti wine sauce) under vaulted ceilings. Large selection of Tuscan wines. *Info*: 2 Vicolo dell'Oro (between Piazza Cisterna and Piazza Duomo). Tel. 0577/941862. Closed Mon. Open daily Easter to Nov. www.ristorantedorando.it. Expensive.

Enoteca Gustavo

San Gimignano can be quite expensive, so visiting a wine bar for a simple snack and drink can be a way to save money. This casual wine bar is another great place to try local wines, especially *Vernaccia di San Gimignano*, the popular local dry white wine. There's a sign in the window boasting "World's Best Bruschetta." That may be an exaggeration, but the *bruschetta* with melted *pecorino* cheese certainly is great with your wine. Other light meals are also available. *Info*: 29 Via San Matteo. Tel. 0577/940057. Inexpensive.

Siena

Enoteca Italiana

This unique *enoteca* (wine bar) is located in the Fortezza Medicea di Santa Barbara, a 16th-century structure. This is Italy's only wine bar sponsored by the country. All of Italy's DOC and DOCG wines are served here (over 400 labels). You can order chees-and-meat plates to accompany your wine, served by the bottle or glass. *Info*: Fortezza Medicea di Santa Barbara on Viale Maccari. Tel. 0577/228811 or 0577/228843. Closed Sun. www.enoteca-italiana.it.

Le Logge

Tuscan dishes at this *osteria* near the Piazza del Campo (one of Italy's most beautiful squares). In the 19th century, this was a simple grocery store. Today, it's a wonderful place to dine, especially if you can score a table outside. Try the *cinghiale* (wild boar). The house specialty is *malfatti all'osteria* (spinach-and-ricotta dumplings in a cream sauce). *Info*: 33 Via del Porrione (a street off of Piazza del Campo). Tel. 0577/48013. Closed Sun and part of Jan. www.osterialelogge.it Moderate – Expensive.

Osteria La Sosta di Violante

Sosta means "break," and this *osteria* is a perfect place to take a break from the crowds. Just a short walk from the Piazza del Campo, you'll find this friendly eatery filled with locals and a few tourists. This isn't fine dining, but there's rustic local fare such as *pici cacio e pepe* (eggless pasta with a sauce of *pecorino* cheese and black pepper) and *risotto al Chianti* (*risotto* in a Chianti wine sauce). *Info*: 115 Via Di Pantaneto. Tel. 0577/43774. Closed Sun. www.lasostadiviolante.it. Inexpensive – Moderate.

Tuscan Wine School

If you have a few hours and want to learn about Italian and Tuscan wines, head here. Classes are taught in English in Siena (and Florence). Two-hour classes with five wines are €40. *Info*: 26 Via Stalloreggi (near Piazza de Conte). Tel. 0577/221704. Closed Sun. www.tuscanwineschool.com (on-line reservations).

Siracusa

Don Camillo

This is a favorite of travelers and locals. You'll sit in vaulted rooms surrounded by wine bottles. Dining here is mostly focused on seafood and Sicilian specialties. You should try the rich and tasty *spaghetti della Sirene* (spaghetti with sea urchin and shrimp in butter). The restaurant is known for its extensive wine list, and you really should try one of the many offerings from Sicily because you most likely won't find these labels at home. *Info*: 96 Via Maestranza. Tel. 0931/67133. Closed Sun. www.ristorantedoncamillosiracusa.it. Moderate – Expensive.

Sicilia in Tavola

This friendly and popular *trattoria* is frequented mostly by locals, and you won't be disappointed by its traditional Sicilian dishes. Start with the fresh *cocktail di gamberetti* (shrimp cocktail) and then move on to *gnocchi di patate con ricci di mare e pistachio* (potato gnocchi with sea urchins and pistachio). Reasonably priced Sicilian wines are featured on the menu, and many selections are from organic wine producers. *Info*: 28 Via Cavour (near Piazza Archimede). Tel. 0392/4610889. Closed Mon. www.siciliaintavola.eu. Moderate.

Caseificio Borderi

Afraid to eat at a food market? Don't be. This eatery at the Ortygia food market has a great selection of cured meats, cheeses, olives, and local wine. Great sandwiches feature meat, marinated mushrooms, sundried tomatoes, mint, cheese, olives, tomatoes, all sprinkled with olive oil and lemon juice. If you're watching your euros, come here and enjoy fresh market food. *Info*: 6 Via Emanuele de Benedictis (Mercato di Ortygia). Tel. 329/9852500. Open 7am-4pm. Closed Sun. www.caseificioborderi.eu. Inexpensive.

Spoleto

Il Tempio del Gusto

Intimate restaurant built on the ruins of an ancient temple.
Glass floor panels let you peer into the wine cellar. Umbria
is Italy's center for truffles, and this restaurant is known for
its dishes featuring *tartufi* (truffles). Excellent *anatra* (duck)
dishes. *Info*: 11 Via Arco di Druso (near Piazza Mercato).
Tel. 0743/47121. Closed Thu. www.iltempiodelgusto.com.
Moderate.

Ristorante Apollinare

You'll dine in candlelight at this former 11th-century monas-
tery. Many of the excellent pasta dishes served here feature
strangozzi, a wheat pasta found in Umbria. In addition to
vegetarian selections, the menu also includes a delicious herb-
roasted *coniglio* (rabbit) served in a black-olive sauce, and tasty
salmone (salmon) and *gamberoni* (shrimp) dishes. The house
red is *Rosso di Montefalco*, a blend of Sangiovese, Sagrantino,
Barbera, Merlot, and Cabernet. *Info*: 14 Via S. Agata (near
Piazza della Liberta) Tel. 0743/223256. Closed Tue.
www.ristoranteapollinare.it. Moderate – Expensive.

Wine and Passion Enoteca Wine Bar

This *enoteca* (wine bar) and wine shop is located on the attractive Piazza Mercato. You're welcomed by Gail Denise, the
owner, who opened the intimate place in 2013. When you order
one of the interesting wines by the glass, you also are served
a small snack. There is an emphasis on Umbrian and Tuscan
wines. A mixture of friendly locals and tourists makes this a
fun experience. *Info*: 21 Piazza Mercato . Tel. 0743/420438.
www.winepassion.it. Moderate.

Taormina

Vecchia Taormina

This long-time favorite eatery serves straight-forward Sicilian
dishes. Try the *pizza alla Norma* (pizza with eggplant and ricotta) or fresh *pesce alla griglia* (grilled fish). In good weather,
sit on the terrace and sip one of the Sicilian wines offered by
the glass or bottle. *Info*: 3 Vico degli Ebrei. Tel. 0942/625589.
Closed Wed and Jan-Feb. Moderate.

Vineria Modi

This steakhouse and wine bar is located just a short walk from the main street Corso Umberto I. Restaurants in Taormina can be overpriced and touristy. Vineria Modi is an exception. You can sit inside or outside and dine on Sicilian specialties. Start with the excellent *insalata di cesare* (Cesar salad) and for your main course, order *spaghetti alle vongole* (spaghetti in clam sauce) or *lombo di maiale* (pork loin). Desserts, and Sicilians are known for their desserts, are made on the premises. Very good selection of local wines. Personable service. *Info*: 13 Via Calapitrulli. Tel. 0942/23658. Closed Wed. Moderate.

Giara

The emphasis is on seafood at this elegant restaurant located in a hillside palazzo in central Taormina. The panoramic terrace has splendid views of the harbor. Traditional Sicilian dishes are given a modern interpretation here, including *ricotta*-stuffed *cannelloni*, swordfish in a tomato sauce, and pork tenderloin in a Marsala wine sauce. *Info*: 1 Vico la Floresta. Tel. 0942/23360. Dinner only. www.lagiarataormina.it. Expensive.

Bam Bar

This is the place in Taormina to experience *granita* (frozen flavored ice similar to a "snow cone"). Here you can try any number of flavors, including *fico* (fig), *limone* (lemon), *mandorla* (almond), and *caffè* (coffee). It's also a great place to have a glass of *prosecco* on the outdoor terrace. *Info*: 45 Via Di Giovanni. Tel. 0942/24355. Open daily. Inexpensive.

Trieste

Buffet Birreria Rudy

Trieste, which remained under United Nations control until 1954, is an interesting mix of Austrian and Italian with a Slavic influence from the former Yugoslav republics. This Austrian/ Bavarian *bierhalle* (beer hall) serves Spaten beer on tap and pasta, soup, and wurst. Known for its *gnocchi* with goulash. *Info*: 32 Via Valdirivo. Tel. 040/639428. Closed Sun. www.buffetrudyspaten.it. Inexpensive.

Gran Malabar

This is a busy, friendly wine bar in the central city. The focus here is on wines produced in the hills of the Friuli-Venezia Giulia region. Your glass (or bottle) of wine will come with cheese, olives, bread, and *prosciutto*. Relax and do some people-watching. *Info*: 6 Piazza San Giovanni. Tel. 040/636226. Closed Sun (evening).

Al Bagatto

Seafood is the specialty at this cozy restaurant a few streets away from the grand Piazza dell'Unità d'Italia. You'll find local favorites like *baccalà* (salt cod) and *branzino* (sea bass). Wine lovers should opt for the *abbinamento vini con 4 calici del territorio* (wines from four nearby regions). The eclectic wine list features selections from lesser-known regional producers. *Info*: 7 Via L. Cadorna. Tel. 040/301771. Closed Sun. No lunch. www.albagatto.it. Moderate – Expensive.

Suban

In the hills two miles north of Trieste, this *trattoria* serves specialties of the Friuli-Venezia Giulia region. It's known for its delectable *gulasch*. You'll find Italian food with a Hungarian, Austrian, and Slovene accent. *Info*: 2 Via Emilio Comici in San Giovanni. Tel. 040/54368. Closed Mon (lunch), Tue and part of Aug. www.suban.it Moderate – Expensive.

Trieste: Cafes
Caffè San Marco

Trieste is famous for its cafes and coffee houses, and this historic café (dating back to 1914) is the king. Some of the original Art Nouveau interior survived severe bombing by Austro-Hungarian troops in World War I. Stepping into the café is almost like stepping back in time. James Joyce used to be a frequent visitor. Dine on local specialties like *jota* (thick bean-and-sauerkraut soup), Italian food like *lasagna*, and even hamburgers. The menu is just as international as Trieste can be. *Info*: 18 Via Cesare Battisti. Tel. 040/0641724. Closed Mon. www.caffesanmarcotrieste.eu. Moderate.

Caffè Degli Specchi

This café on Piazza dell'Unità d'Italia, Trieste's great square, opened in 1839. It has an interesting history, as the British commandeered it during World War II. It's a favorite destination for coffee during the day. There's also a gourmet restaurant on the premises. Score a table on the square, have a snack and a drink, and enjoy some great people-watching. It feels like a Viennese coffee house has been transported to Trieste. *Info*: Piazza dell'Unità d'Italia. Tel. 040/661973. Open daily. www.caffespecchi.it.

Turin
Al Bicerin
Founded in 1763, this tiny café is a great place to stop when visiting the market at the nearby Piazza della Repubblica (Mon to Sat 8am-2pm). Order a *bicerin*, a combination of chocolate, coffee, and cream. *Info*: 5 Piazza della Consolata. Tel. 011/4369325. Closed Wed and Aug. www.bicerin.it. Moderate.

Da Cianci Piola Caffé
Piedmontese food at reasonable prices at this friendly and crowded *trattoria*. When choosing something from the chalkboard menu, try a delicious *coniglio* (rabbit) dish. Tables spill onto the charming square in good weather. *Info*: 9B Largo IV Marzo (near Piazza Castello). Tel. 338/8767003. Open daily. Inexpensive.

Ruràl
Foodies will love this modern restaurant with an open kitchen. The restaurant is part of the "Slow Food" movement (which emphasizes locally grown products and regional cuisine). The wine list focuses on lesser-known wines from the Piedmont region. The menu features such dishes as *verdure alla griglia* (a plate of fresh grilled green vegetables), *risotto alla barbabietola, gorgonzola e nocciole* (risotto with beets, gorgonzola, and hazelnuts), and *costata di manzo* (rib steak), and all the ingredients are from farmers and breeders from the Piedmont region. *Info*: 16 Via San Dalmazzo. Tel. 011/2478470. Closed Sun. www.ristoranterural.it. Moderate –Expensive.

Baratti e Milano
This historic café dates back to 1858 and is famous for its chocolates, especially *gianduiotti* (hazelnut chocolates). You'll feel like you stepped back in time while you indulge in the pastries, ice cream, coffee, and drinks here. It's located in the

glass-covered Galleria Subalpina. *Info*: 29 Piazza Castello. Tel.
011/4407138. Closed Mon. www.barattiemilano.it.

Eataly Torino Lingotto
The Turin location of this large food emporium is located in a
former factory building. The "Slow Food" movement (which
emphasizes locally grown products and regional cuisine) began
in the area, and there's a large section devoted to the movement. You'll find cheese, meats, homemade pasta, sauces, and
pastries. Wines from Piedmont are also featured here, so it's a
great place to try Barbera, Nebbiolo, and Moscato. *Info*: 230
Via Nizza (From central Turin, take the metro to Lingotto stop).
Tel. 011/19506801. Open daily 10am-10.30pm. www.eataly.net

Venice
Santa Croce neighborhood
Antico Giardinetto
Friendly, informal, family-run *osteria*. Try the *filetto di
manzo ai 3 pepi* (filet of beef with pepper sauce) or *costolette
d'agnello Toscano scottadito* (Tuscan roasted lamb chops).
There are many seafood options on the menu, including *soutè
di cozze e vongole* (sautéed mussels and clams). Decent house
red wine, too. *Info*: 2253 Santa Croce, Calle dei Morti (near
Campo San Cassiano). Rialto vaporetto. Tel. 041/722882.
www.anticogiardinetto.it. Closed Mon and part of Jan. No
lunch. Moderate – Expensive.

Il Refolo
This pizzeria/restaurant is on a picturesque square overlooking
the church of San Giacomo dell'Orio. Customers dock their
boats along the patio for take-out. Try the pizza topped with
a local specialty, *castraure* (the first floral shoot of the artichoke). One pizza on the menu features roasted figs and *proscuitto*. *Info*: 1459 Santa Croce. Campiello del Piovan (Campo
San Giacomo dell'Orio). Riva di Biasio or San Stae vaporetto.
Tel. 041/5240016. Closed Mon, Tue (lunch), and Dec-Mar.
Moderate.

San Marco neighborhood
Da Ivo
Beautiful restaurant serving Venetian (and Tuscan) special-
ties. Try the delicious *bistecca alla Fiorentina* (T-bone steak).

We came here before celebrities like George Clooney came here. So, he's just copying us. *Info*: 1809 San Marco. Calle dei Fuseri (near Campo S. Luca). Tel. 041/5285004. www.ristorantedaivo.it. Closed Sun and Jan. Vaporetto: San Marco. Expensive – Very Expensive.

Enoteca al Volto

This wine bar has wooden tables and chairs, wine labels as wallpaper, an impressive wine list, and simple Venetian fare. Try the *ravioloni di asparagi con capesante e fiori di zucca* (asparagus ravioli with scallops and zucchini flowers). A great deal. *Info*: 4081 San Marco. Calle Cavalli (between the Grand Canal and Salizzada San Luca). Rialto vaporetto. Tel. 041/5228945. www.enotecaalvolto.com. Open daily. Inexpensive – Moderate.

Da Mamo

Pasta, pizza, and large salads at this cozy and casual *trattoria*. Good value. Try the *pizza diavola* with tomato, mozzarella, and spicy salami. Although it's a bit corny, they have a *pizze zodiaco* menu featuring a pizza named after the twelve signs of the zodiac. *Pizza Toro* (Taurus) is topped with tomato, mozzarella, sausage, brie, and pepperoni. *Info*: 5251 San Marco. Calle Stagneri (near Campo San Bartolomio). Rialto vaporetto. Tel. 041/5236583. www.damamo.it. Open daily. Moderate.

Vino Vino

Popular wine bar and restaurant (near the Teatro La Fenice) serving typical Venetian cuisine and offering 200 Italian and imported wines by the bottle or glass. Try the local specialty, *sarde in saor* (sardines in a sweet-and-sour sauce). *Info*: 2007A San Marco. Ponte delle Veste (between La Fenice and via XXII Marzo). Tel. 041/2417688. Open daily. Vaporetto: S. Maria del Giglio. Inexpensive – Moderate.

Castello neighborhood
Dal Moro's - Fresh Pasta To Go

This unassuming and hard to find take-out place is hugely popular. Pasta is made fresh on the premises, and you can order any number of sauces. The *arrabbiata* (spicy tomato and herb sauce) is particularly good. A great way to save money in Venice, where dining can be quite expensive. Each serving costs around €7. Despite the crowds, the servers are very friendly. *Info*: 5324 Castello. Calle de la Casseleria. (near the church of Santa Maria Formoso). Tel. 327/8705014 Open Mon-Sat noon-8:30pm. No credit cards. www.facebook.com/DalMorosFreshPastaToGo. Closed Sun. Inexpensive.

Al Mascaron

You might have to sit next to strangers (mostly tourists) at long tables in this unpretentious restaurant/bar. The food is straightforward Venetian. Try the deep-fried *calamari*. The specialty here is *spaghetti allo scoglio* (spaghetti with lobster, shrimp, and scallops). *Info*: 5225 Castello. Calle Lunga Santa Maria Formosa (near the Campo Santa Maria Formosa). Rialto vaporetto. Tel. 041/5225995. www.osteriamascaron.it. Closed Sun and Jan. No credit cards. Moderate.

Oliva Nera

Expect a warm welcome from owners Dino and Isabella at this small, charming *osteria*. Try the *ossobuco* (braised veal shank), *baccalà* (salt cod), or dishes served with *nero di seppia* (black squid ink). You might even leave with a complimentary bottle of the house olive oil. *Info*: 3417/3447 Castello. From Riva degli Schiavoni (on the waterfront), turn onto Calle della Pietà, left on Calle Bosello to Salizada dei Greci. San Zaccaria vaporetto. Tel. 041/5222170. www.olivanera.com. Closed Wed. Dinner only. Moderate – Expensive.

Al Covo

Fresh Venetian specialties (especially seafood) at this small *osteria*. Try the *fritto misto* (mixed deep-fried fish). *Info*: 3968 Castello. Campiello della Pescaria (off of Riva degli Schiavoni). Arsenale vaporetto. Tel. 041/5223812. www.ristorantealcovo.com. Closed Wed, Thu, Jan, and part of Aug. No lunch Mon and Tue. No credit cards. Moderate – Expensive.

Cannaregio neighborhood

Malibran

Intimate restaurant, complete with Venetian-glass chandeliers, near the Rialto Bridge. Italian dishes and homemade pizza. The interesting *pizza della casa* has tomatoes, mozzarella, ham, mushrooms, salami, artichokes, and an egg on top. Pasta dishes include *tortellini panna, proscuitto, e funghi* (tortellini pasta with cream, ham, and mushrooms). *Info*: 5864 Cannaregio. Off of Salizzada San Giovanni Grisostomo and overlooking the Teatro Malibran. Rialto vaporetto. Tel. 041/5228028. www.hotelmalibran.com. Open daily. Moderate.

Vini da Gigio

Wine bar and *osteria* serving Venetian specialties and home-made pasta. Delicious *gnocchi*. There are two seatings on Sat and Sun (7pm and 9pm). *Info*: 3628A Cannaregio. Fondamenta San Felice (just off the Strada Nuova). Cá d'Oro vaporetto. Tel. 041/5285140. Closed Mon, Tue, part of Jan and part of Aug. Moderate – Expensive.

Dorsoduro neighborhood

Ai Gondolieri

Not for seafood lovers. This restaurant serves meat dishes like *ossobuco di vitello* (braised veal shank). Try the creamy *risotto con funghi porcini* (risotto with porcini mushrooms). Delicious *fiori di zucca* (zucchini flowers filled w/cheese, then battered and fried). *Info*: 366 Dorsoduro. Fondamenta dell'Ospedaleto (near the Guggenheim Museum at Fondamenta Venier dai Leoni). Accademia vaporetto. Tel. 041/5286396. www.aigondolieri.it. Closed Tue. Moderate – Expensive.

La Bitta

In a small storefront, this family-owned restaurant and wine bar focuses on meat dishes (often accompanied by grilled vegetables). The *porchetta* (roast suckling pig stuffed with herbs), served with a horseradish sauce, is delicious. The menu also features dishes served with *peverada* (a spicy sauce with chicken livers and anchovies). Desserts include an excellent *panna cotta* (rich cream custard). Wine comes in a bottle, but you only pay for what you've consumed. End your meal with *grappa*. *Info*: 2753A Dorsoduro. Calle Lunga San Barnaba (off of Campo San Barnaba). Ca' Rezzonico vaporetto. Tel. 041/5230531. Closed Sun and part of Jul. No lunch. No credit cards. Moderate.

Venice: Ciccheti Bars

Ciccheti, the Venetian version of *tapas*, are served at *bàcari* (small, local bars) with glasses of wine. Starting at as little as €1, you'll pay a fraction of the cost that you would at a café. It's a great way to eat on a budget. Here are a few places to try *ciccheti*. (Most are near the Rialto vaporetto)

Cantina do Mori

429 San Polo (on the San Polo side of Rialto Bridge, walk to end of the market stalls, turn left and then immediately right). Tel. 041/5225401. Closed Sun. Try the *melanzane alla parmigiana* (eggplant parmesan).

Bancogiro

122 Campo San Giacometto (west end of Rialto Bridge along the Grand Canal). Tel. 041/5232061. Closed Mon. www.osteriabancogiro.it. Try the *selezione di formaggi* (cheese plate).

Al Mercà

213 Campo Cesare Battisti, San Polo. On a picturesque square in Rialto Markets area (off of Fondamenta Riva Olio). Tel. 347/1002583. Try the *robiola* (soft, mild, and slightly sweet cheese).

Cantina Do Spade

30125 San Polo, 19 Calle Do Spade, On a narrow alleyway near Campo Beccarie (near the Rialto Bridge). Tel. 041/5210583. www.cantinadospade.com. No lunch Tue. Try the *calamari fritti* (fried squid).

All'Arco

436 San Polo, Calle Arco (lunch only). Near the Rialto Bridge (off of Ruga del Spezieri). Tel. 041/5205666. Closed Sun. Try the *acciughe* (anchovies).

Trattoria Ca d'Oro alla Vedova

3912 Cannaregio, Calle de Pistor (at Ramo D. Ca d'Oro off of Strada Nova). Tel. 041/5285324. Closed Thu and Sun (lunch). Try *polpetta di carne* (meatball).

Cantinone Gia' Schiavi
992 Fondamenta Nani. Tel. 041/5230034. Located in the
Accademia neighborhood (near Calle Contarini Corfu). Closed
Sun. Try the *baccalà* (salted cod).

Rialto Bridge (Rialto vaporetto): 7am-1pm, Mon-Sat.
Via Garibaldi (Arsenale vaporetto): Mornings, Mon-Fri.

Caffè Florian
Piazza San Marco (St. Mark's Square) is home to this elegant
and expensive café. It has been in business since 1720, and it's
worth the splurge to sit and listen to the orchestra in one of the
world's loveliest squares. In fact, you'll pay more when the
orchestra performs. When the weather isn't great, you can sit
inside surrounded by mirrors, statues, and frescoes. Expect to
pay at least €20 for a Bellini (*prosecco* and peach nectar). *Info*:
56 Piazza San Marco. Tel. 041/5205641. Closed Wed in winter.
Open daily 9am-midnight. Vaporetto: San Marco.

Al Prosecco
You can't come to Italy and not sample *prosecco*. This sparkling white wine will tickle your tongue and quench your thirst,
especially on a warm Venetian night. Great terrace and simple
cichetti (the Venetian version of Spanish *tapas*). A glass of *prosecco* begins at €4 and goes up from there. *Info*: 1503 Campo
San Giacomo de l'Orio (Santa Croce). Tel. 041/5240222.
Closed Sun, Aug, and Jan. www.alprosecco.com. Vaporetto:
San Stae.

Harry's Bar
Travelers continue to flock to Harry's Bar just west of St.
Mark's Square. Although dinner is extremely expensive (and
many complain not worth the cost), most come to have a martini or delicious Bellini (sparkling *prosecco* and peach nectar)
at the bar. The drink will cost you around €20, so drink it slow-
ly! If it was good enough for Ernest Hemingway and Truman
Capote, it should be good enough for you. *Info*: 1323 Calle
Vallaresso. Tel 041/5285777. Open daily. www.cipriani.com.

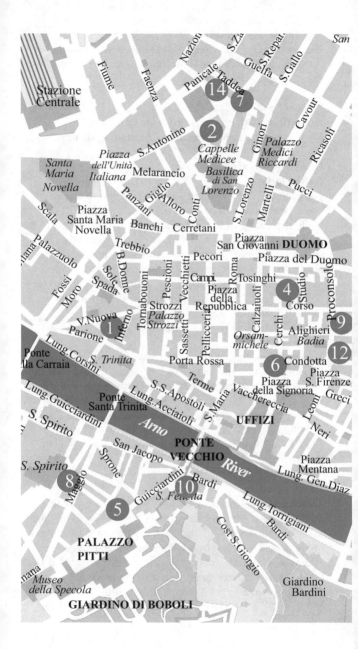

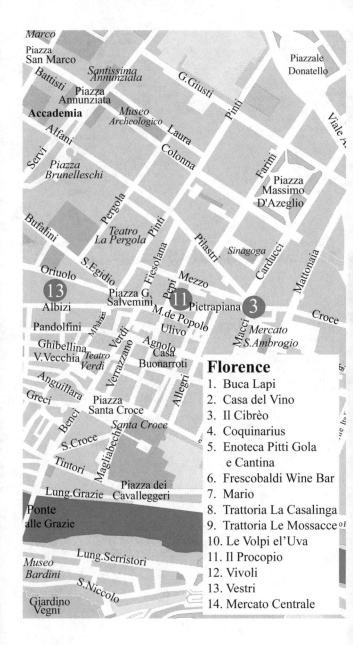

Florence

1. Buca Lapi
2. Casa del Vino
3. Il Cibrèo
4. Coquinarius
5. Enoteca Pitti Gola
   e Cantina
6. Frescobaldi Wine Bar
7. Mario
8. Trattoria La Casalinga
9. Trattoria Le Mossacce
10. Le Volpi el'Uva
11. Il Procopio
12. Vivoli
13. Vestri
14. Mercato Centrale

Tuscany and Umbria

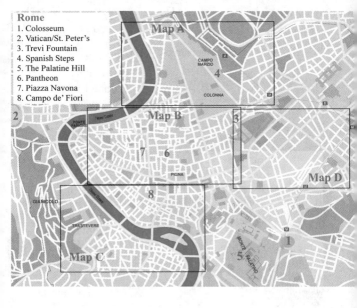

Rome
1. Colosseum
2. Vatican/St. Peter's
3. Trevi Fountain
4. Spanish Steps
5. The Palatine Hill
6. Pantheon
7. Piazza Navona
8. Campo de' Fiori

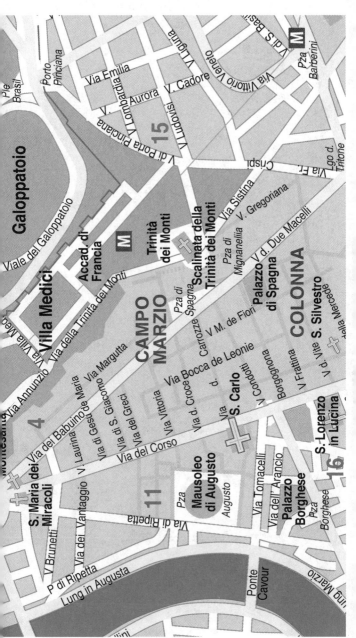

Rome Map B - Piazza Navona/Pantheon/
Trevi Fountain

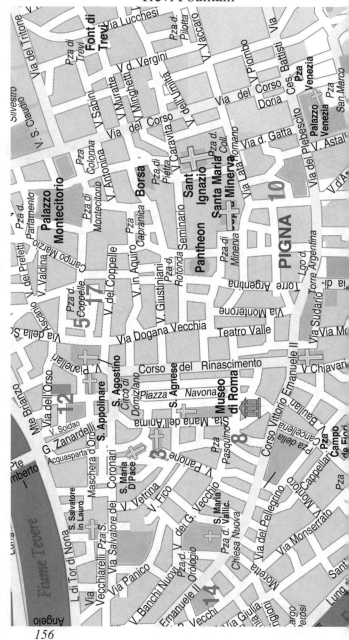

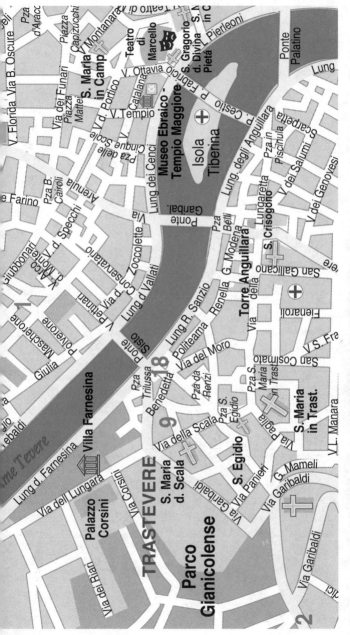

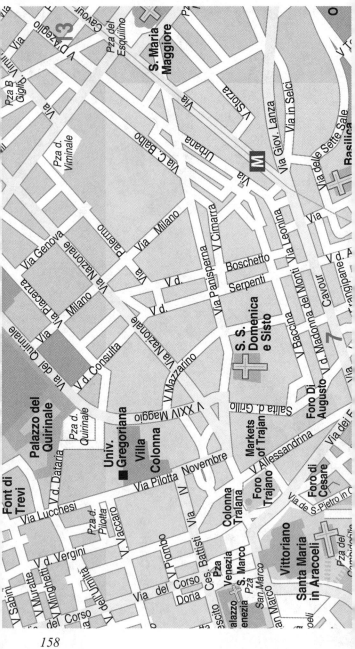

Restaurants by Location

Descriptions of restaurants in the cities listed here can be found on the page number following each city.

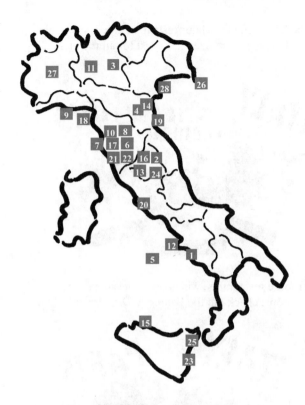

Also available from
Open Road Publishing

The best menu translator/restaurant guides available!
Handy, pocket-sized ... a must for all travelers.

For more restaurants, wine bars, wine shops, and food
shops, check out the *Wining & Dining* guides!

Published by Open Road Publishing
Distributed by Simon & Schuster
www.eatndrink.com
www.openroadguides.com